HORSE'S NECK

ff

PETE
TOWNSHEND

Horse's Neck

faber and faber
LONDON · BOSTON

First published in 1985
by Faber and Faber Limited
3 Queen Square London WC1N 3AU
First published in Faber Paperbacks in 1986

Typeset by Goodfellow & Egan Ltd Cambridge
Printed in Great Britain by
Butler & Tanner Ltd, Frome and London
All rights reserved

© Pete Townshend, 1985

British Library Cataloguing in Publication Data

Townshend, Pete
Horse's neck.
I. Title
828'.91408   PR6070.09/

ISBN 0-571-13873-X

CONTENTS

This collection of prose and verse was written between 1979 and 1984.

I have never wanted simply to tell my own story. But I have tried here to attend to a wide range of feelings. So the collection opens with a dimly remembered story of infancy. It closes with a vivid glimpse of the very near future.

My mother features in this book, but her character changes constantly because this "mother" is many mothers, many teachers.

Each story deals with one aspect of my struggle to discover what beauty really is.

Pete Townshend
June 1984

THIRTEEN

What did I do for him?
I gave him life
I foresaw the danger
I prepared him
I hardened him
I nurtured his femininity
I praised his maleness
I deliberately failed him
I scorned his team-mates
I judged his fellows
I was his conscience
I was his inquisitor
Gave him his freedom
Encouraged his fantasies
Sneered at his inadequacies
I lost him to another
But I produced him
I conceived him
I breast-fed him first
I screamed with him first
I adored him first
I rejected him first
What did I do for him?
Only what any mother would have done.

I remember the noise of the wind moving through the coarse
grass, the sanctity of our protected spot never threatened
even by the sea before us, blue-grey and green. I remember
the sky, fluffy with clouds like breath over frost. I know that I
could not possibly have been alone; and yet, looking back
through the veils of childhood, I recall only a strange feeling
of autonomy, but with no sensation of isolation. I was secure.

11

I was to be "alone" often, and remember waiting, but I was always sure that they would come eventually.

The dunes were rich and spreading, billowing and easy like dusty sheets. The air felt both cool and warm at once; a breeze disguised the confusion, and the grey haze lightly accented the precision of the northern English summer weather.

The beach at Filey was a Northumbrian miracle; sandy hollows exposed wind-eroded wombs to a sometimes raging sea. At certain moments you could believe that no one had ever run their fingers through the golden dust, or that no cigarette had ever been discarded. The exploring hand of an inquisitive child would belie that fancy. Even at the water's edge the flotsam of civilization floated gently home. Between the waves the heads of seals would bob, their whiskered noses inspecting the shore. Nearby, a more complete invasion threatened: holiday camps and railways, ice-cream parlours and penny arcades at Whitley Bay. Yet in the hollow of a sand dune, a child could well be on a desert island.

It seems there are always a thousand surviving, aching memories, even from the cushioned emotions of the child fresh from the womb. Proust wrote of the fragility of a boy dependent on his mother's sweet kiss. Joyce pondered on the power of a mother's embrace: fellows at school asked the young hero if his mother kissed him goodnight. The answer, whether yes or no, always brought laughter from the crowd, and a curious shame to his heart.

I too waited for a kiss, but I was too young to know exactly what I expected or desired. My recollection is of a dreamy afternoon, languorous and drawn out, without detail or punctuation. Then suddenly across the shining strip of surf-glazed beach, the sound of horses splashing and thudding on the sand by the water's edge caught my attention. Two chestnuts veered away from the foam towards me and their young riders raced, in a spray of sand and sweat, to be the first to reach me.

The woman's auburn hair was pulled back in a bun, her

eyes gleamed and her smiling complexion shone as she, the winner, gazed down at me. I felt exposed but sure that my nakedness would soon be covered. Then the man rode close and manoeuvred his mount, his hair swept back, his face handsome and sunburned. He wore a check shirt with rolled up sleeves, and splendid handmade brown riding boots cut close to his skin. He pulled gently at the reins and brought his frothing horse to rest. My mother and father had completed my world for me.

As though riding out of the sea and up to the dunes where I played, they were breaking the spell of my loneliness. Now I knew what I waited for, what I missed, but they stayed only for a minute and were gone, galloping off again laughing and waving. This is my earliest memory.

Once, when I talked about this to my mother in later life, trying to express the depth of my emotions as a child, she replied that I must be mistaken. The only time we had all been together on the dunes at Filey was when I was only one month into my second year. But I do remember, and to this day I have never felt inclined to ride a horse.

HORSES

I remember, once, realizing how magnificent was the concept of the pantomime horse. How the front end belonged to the back end. How the back end bloody well followed the front end in darkness and humiliation. I longed, for a second, to be that man trapped inside the coloured horse.

I dreamed, once, that I flew over a ruined church set on the edge of a hill. Nothing remained except the foundations of the crypt and the cellar. A horse had slipped on the stony ground from the hillside into the basement ruin and couldn't escape. The terrified animal was running in a mindless circle. Above was the blue sky. One remaining wall with a stained-glass window stood high. The floor of the crypt was strewn with rocks and was full of puddles. The horse's fetlocks were bleeding, its body slowly starving. I flew on, helpless to assist. It was a terrible dream and seemed portentous.

The circling horse was an oblique warning that I would repeat the same mistake eternally. Would the law of averages allow it? Can anything continue without change? Nothing else in nature behaves so consistently and rigidly as a human being in pursuit of hell.

In my dream I wanted to close my eyes, to pretend that I was asleep, feigning cocaine madness or brandy oblivion. The sun was shining in a quiet, underhand manner. I could almost imagine a mist before my eyes and yet there was no mist, just a feeling of something going slightly wrong, and of excitement and anticipation.

They say men on a battlefield experience the same mood just before a charge. Suddenly life seems worth living, birds sing as if for the first time and even the subtleties of nature, like the rustling of leaves, become important and demanding. Lovers speak of it too. Imagine a boy holding the hand of a girl, the spark of contact enhancing their every step through the park. The cock is erect, hard and insistent beneath unwashed jeans, the sweat is beaded on the brow and yet there is no chance of those lovers conjoining.

That was the feeling. In my dream I walked into the village alone. It was apparently inhabited and normal. One cottage attracted me immediately. It reminded me at first of the houses in *The Country of the Blind*. There was something welcoming and friendly about it, something warm and natural. The birds sang and the leaves rustled.

The door of the cottage was open, and surrounded by flowering clematis. The walls of the cottage were of grey stone. Imagine a Cotswold village, where every lintel, every window frame, every garden wall, in an area over a hundred miles square, is hewn from the same quarry and strata, extracted from the same instant of history. There you will see the colour of this structure. It belonged. It was, and it had been. It was in context, and it felt correct.

Faced with the beckoning doorway and yet dismayed by that strange feeling of anticipation, I wanted to fall back into oblivion. I would happily have gone to my fate in darkness.

As I walked through the door of the cottage, pushing and finding it open, I confronted an empty parlour. The house was devoid of furniture, deserted and abandoned, except that the tiny room was occupied by another horse. Its head was not quite touching the low ceiling, but there was still no way the creature could raise its head without bumping the plaster cornice. The animal was pure white like a death mask. The correct term for a white horse is "grey", which is intended to signify that no horse is pure white, not even an albino. But this creature seemed flawlessly white; a symbol of purity.

I have to pause and take another glass of Calvados, another wheeze on a foul cigarette before continuing. At moments like this I feel like a night owl. I shall retire in an hour and thrash about the bed, pulling the sheets from my wife, leaving her naked and cold. I'll wake every half an hour or so and switch on the lamp and scribble notes on the back of envelopes, or in the flyleaf of a current novel. In the morning

I'll wonder what the hell I was thinking of; I'm sure you know the feeling.

Confronting the white horse I put out my hand and brushed hard down the flank as if to smooth away the mark of a girth strap. As I did so, the skin fell away, and the dry white bones of the rib cage appeared. Beneath the ribs, living within the body of the horse, moved a massive snake. Its skin shone green and blue. It was bloated and overfed; full of the heart, the liver, and the intestines of my perfect horse, my symbol of purity. It moved within the body of the horse in a circle.

I wish it were really a dream. The village exists, the horse exists. I suppose I win in the end. How can I fail? With infinite dream potential I can believe in everything. This is a gift from God, a presentation of his grace. If it arrives with the package torn I can't argue. I'm ready to be humiliated, to suffer, to go through whatever I need to go through. I won't betray God or his world.

Another cigarette, then to bed, please God to dream again, to be refreshed. There is no blood like the blood that flows within one's own body. No dreams like those that spark from one's own mind. Nothing is necessary except a dream. A dream can set off reality; the smoke ring rises vertically, perfectly round and in equipoise, then wavers and collapses.

Nothing has anything to do with you or me.

THE PACT

I found him staring at the river outside his house. He had been reading a letter. Without speaking he looked up and smiled, then handed me the envelope casually. I read the feminine script:

To my secret love,

You asked me why I have been so licentious, and why I have seemed so uncaring towards you. I will try to explain.

Because I am beautiful I am expected to be mindless; I am to take an ugly, intellectual lover or someone old and rich. My long hair and even features lead me irrevocably into affairs with dozens of men. Each one tries to decide what it is I really need from life. If I interrupt these suitors while their philosophical flow is unleashed, they become deeply shaken. So much so, that when I apologize, and ask them to continue, they cannot.

When I awaken and look in the mirror, I admit that the first emotion I feel is the joy of relief. It doesn't matter where I am I might have risen from the bed of a complete stranger, or from my little bed at the home of my father and his brothers, or in my own tatty bedsitting room, but my reflected face is like a reward. I feel as though I have been born again – rich.

I'm not arrogant in my self-confidence; I decry my fleshy nose; regret my sometimes overweight figure, but it gives me pleasure to know that I am exceptional, and that I never had to work for a second to achieve that.

I look for beauty in others, I feel that my aura needs to be complemented, not balanced. And so I don't like to be compared to a greying, balding old man at my side. (He is regarded as a lecherous fool. But what of me? Even if I happened to love this old man, I am ridiculed, scorned like a whore. My beauty is often a burden.)

I know you dream of me. You further idealize me in your reverie. My ankles, a little thick, become delicate and smooth; my hair, a little straight, becomes mobile and light. Sometimes you write to me possessively: *I could make you happy*, or *I can't live without you*. At other times you write in an off-hand way: *Saw you in the street the other day, you looked well, I'm well. What are you up to?* Sometimes you attack me: *You think you are so special that you can ignore me.* That sort of thing.

I am special. To be beautiful is to be lucky; to be lucky is to have received grace; to receive grace means you have been chosen. Too late now to turn back. I am beautiful and must suffer the consequences.

I am never entirely sure what a man wants from me. That is why I have always preferred horses. I can't entirely trust a man who tells me he appreciates my looks, because there are so many others with good looks.

It can be a curiously claustrophobic experience being brought up as your mother's doll: pampered, dressed up and brushed. Father always refused to play such feminine and childish games. He said they were shallow pursuits. He neglected me.

Then as I grew up I felt father take pride in my effect on men; he now feels a power, through me, over those younger and more vital than himself. Imbued with this new value I become interesting to him again.

But that interest annoys my mother who is growing tired and tawdry. She is jealous and suspects the worst kind of sexual desire in my father or his brothers. It's always me that suffers.

Sometimes I am afraid to hold myself up to my full height. I don't want to flaunt my attributes or look arrogant. My bosom thrust out, my full head of hair blowing free, I feel devastating. This doesn't always suit my mood. If I wish to appear modest and unassuming for any reason, it's difficult. My only privacy is in total isolation.

But there are so many rewards. Most wonderful is the freedom of choice beauty ensures. I don't have to seize and hang on to the first lover of consequence in my life. I can take hundreds of lovers. I suppose I've passed over a few compatible partners like this, but there are so many lonely people looking for a prize like me.

Then there are more disadvantages. It can be utterly agonizing when my natural assets have no effect on a man. I am so used to being the centre of attention, of being fawned upon and fêted, that when I am ignored or rejected I have little wisdom of such experiences to fall back on.

I only want one true love. I am like every other human being in that respect. But God-given talent must not be wasted. So I am flirtatious and capricious. In this way, just as when I am riding an enormous stallion, I am completely in command.

I think I might use my looks to steal someone else's cherished partner. Why should I have to experiment? Let someone else weed out the inadequate and selfish lovers. If I see someone who has proved themselves once already in love, that is good enough for me. Why should I take risks?

My requirements then are simple; I want a young partner, but someone who has already established that they can give themselves completely in a relationship. My beauty must draw them away from any commitment.

I insist that my partner be as lucky as I am so that we might suffer equally as our luck runs slowly out until our death.

But most of all I insist that my partner be beautiful, not so perfect as to outshine me, but beautiful enough – so that my son shall also be beautiful.

I handed the letter back to him.

"Who wrote this?"

"It's from my mother."

"Where did you get it?" I asked.

"I visited her this morning. She seems to be a bit unhinged. I think the letter was written for me."

"But she's writing like a young girl to a spurned lover – justifying herself."

"Interesting, isn't it?" he said as he turned back towards the river.

CHAMPAGNE ON THE TERRACES

The homing ritual remained unchanged, a hidden foundation throughout his brick-built marriage, he stalked his childhood path down the amber-glinting street towards his house. He was tired as usual, his limbs felt tightly roped. He was fulfilled as usual, heart ginger-warm; but the feeling on this particular evening was different, like finding a new finger among the familiar five. Everything felt slightly strange.

"I'm home!" He walked through his low front door, into the place that he and his family had shared for over twelve years. It was a clean, bright home, full of memories: Christmases, hotpots, and crackling fires. Once he had been a serious drinker, causing crashing outbursts as he staggered mean and black-hearted from his evening at the rail. Now he took off his coat and sat down to a neat tea prepared by his wife. Her eyes shone at her weary, bread-winning fool, and saw a heroic soldier. It drove her mad not to know whom he really took himself to be.

Their life appeared like the wind-scattered leaves of a cheap, complimentary calendar – at first serenely pastoral and secure, then crumpled and naked; full of brazen, threatening bosoms. It had been equally strange for them both over the last two years. All of a sudden the mute and frozen confrontation that occurs in every family's life had happened. She had been unable to deal with his drinking. She tended to blame drink for all his extremes in behaviour.

Looking at her, he knew that his extremes had been his way to keep her love and interest in him alive and fresh. He adored her, but he dreaded her in his heart, this was so different to the way he had buffeted her in his arms. He whip-panned between true recognition of her perfect soul and his steam-kettle lust for her down-pillow bosom. Her eyes tolerated him, praised him, rebuked him. He hid from them wearing his body like a spacesuit. Then the shy smile would be sweetly won, the firm persuasive lips would seek out their nipple-sweet opposites and lovers would blend smoothly like butter and flour cooking in a roux.

And yet now, looking back on those crimson days of his alcoholic fury, he felt disgusted at himself. He thought about some of the things that had happened, things he had done, events so out of key with reality that they might as well have been dreams.

He was taken by a friend to a new, white railway station somewhere in London. Everything about the station was normal, though curved and plastic chrome like a modern vacuum cleaner. A sibilant hiss caressed the body-temperature air; a fragrance of neoteric sensuality buzzed; a synthetic summer day was being piped into the void. It was a weird system. The traveller, reclining back, occupied a small capsule with only his head raised a little so he could see forward. The seat, or couch, that the traveller enjoyed enveloped the body like a half cocoon. He floated, like a suckling babe being bathed in a little tub. The sensation was sensuous and skin-tingling, an experience of nudity surrounded in flesh; muscled bone cradled between warm breasts.

The capsule itself sat at the top of a chute which faced a tunnel that offered an opening like a throat directly into the earth. The tunnel was shaped to be an exact fit for the capsule. The traveller could see forward into the tube, which was illuminated through the walls, as though the whole tube was itself a giant fibre-optic. The glow was alternately gold then silver, soft yet intense.

The capsule flung itself exhilaratingly forward for a tremendous fairground ride down into the bowels of the city. Every now and then a violent junction would be encountered and the capsule would career with accuracy and assurance around the bend on to its new course. The occupant felt secure yet helpless, like a papoose propelled inside a warhead.

The journey ended suddenly with an accident. At a junction his capsule met another. His vehicle stopped and he realized, lying prone and stiff, that he was trapped. Claustrophobia crept up until he felt as if he had exploded. Time stopped like death. The air was stale in an instant. His awakening had been shocking.

His wife had blamed his heavy drinking before he went back to sleep. And yet in real life he had seen and experienced worse. He had dreamed worse.

He visited a sleazy massage parlour in Amsterdam. He went in to find rooms full of people engaged in every kind of weird perversion. Men and women copulated; business men in shirt-tails lay with aryan fledgling girls with unbroken porcelain skin; a woman like a courtier, an old Dame dressed in lace, sat at a dining table with a wine bottle between her legs, a candle burning low before her; a man surrounded by flirting and tickling boys who were aroused like captive monkeys.

He wandered through the bordello looking for the coquetry of his own, impossible fantasy. He found what he didn't know he wanted: a horizontal bed like a dentist's chair. It was covered with old food scraps left behind from an earlier perverted game. It had levers to alter its height and elevation. The contraption was ancient and tatty, but the aroma in the room was fruity and tart. The scent suggested pagan temples. He lay on the bed and a girl with a dirty face and tangled hair entered. She was dressed in a hippyesque leather costume and was holding a battered old piece of hospital equipment. Her costume covered her breasts and belly but as she fussed around him, gently settling him on his stomach, legs spreadeagled, he caught glimpses of her buttocks between corset and garters. A clump of hair like a bush revealed itself when she leaned down. She held up a rubber tube, with a dark plastic nozzle. He realized he was about to be flushed out like some constipated farmyard animal. To his surprise he enjoyed the experience, but did he really speak the name of a girl in his sleep? Had he been asleep?

It could have been a dream – but in real life he had done worse.

In the last few months of his wriggling abstinence, every human being and all natural things appeared with auras. There were halos around buildings, even around bits of paper fluttering in the street.

Now a gripping optimism filled him, hardening in the pit of his chest. He felt the petals of his heart opening as his shoulders widened and his eyes gazed at the green miniature jungle-world around him. His mind was quick and pleased with itself. He surprised himself regularly. He remembered the sensation of sensation. But an ache tore bitterly at his temperate satisfaction; only his strength, his railtrack stubbornness, kept him from smoke-filled taverns. He missed the inconsequent language, the half-slurred jokes of fools with golden hearts and eyes. He longed for the crumbling bouquet of walnut-tart beer, sprung from oak barrels. How could he abandon either what he had once known or what he now knew?

He was only twenty-nine, yet he still thought readily of the days when he would be dead, retired, or senile. He had always felt old. He wasn't obsessed by any of this, just aware that everyone is eventually dead. He was a tall man, attracted to similar types, married to a tallish-looking woman with two string-bean kids. (His sons were young but clever, and street-wise, and popular too, he liked to think. They played a good game of football. They were tough but also compassionate: good qualities for growing men.) His face was typical of the workers at his factory, slightly lined, a tiny glint of bitterness in the corner of his steel-blue eyes. His hands were large but delicate and clean, his job involved glass tubes for scientific and medical purposes. Tubes, pipes, funnels, test tubes, files, pipettes and flasks.

He loved being in Wales and loved the Welsh above all others. Not completely unique in this respect he preferred football to rugby. But the Welsh sang. Not just in choirs but also in their conversation; their chosen words and their accents had charmed him since boyhood.

His life's real passion, however, had been drink. He had

often said that he couldn't respect a man that didn't drink. In truth there was something more. He didn't trust a man that didn't drink. His wife knew she had a problem with him because she hated booze herself and couldn't cope with much of it anyway. She certainly wasn't the hearty type who could handle a lusty lush sobbing to be returned to the womb in the middle of the night. Yet this suited him because he didn't approve of women who drank. Men were born to drink, according to his ethos; women didn't need it.

Now he sipped his tea.

"Since you've been on the wagon all you do is sit and dream," his wife laughed. Her face glowed like a successful angler as she buttered his toast for him and arranged dainty cakes. She was adjusting him in her keepnet; he was in the rushing river, but not of it; dangerous but contained. She was relieved by his temperance, even though he had slowed down as a lover. She had tossed and turned sometimes, yearning for awakenings like those she had known in the past, his face between her legs, laughing and obstreperous. Or her rising up through a dream to his lips on hers, his familiar tobacco breath smiling her awake, rolling her, smoothing her, delighting her. She missed his sudden weight on her vacant body, prefaced by the barking dog signalling his return.

"I dream at night too," he said, "sometimes I wish you were there, you might learn something to your advantage about me." He hardly looked up, but smiled gently. She smiled back at him, in this second he was forgiven everything:

"And what would I learn? Like any other man you dream of bloody women and not much else." He got up and walked towards his chair by the fire.

"I dream of women." He grabbed a cigarette and lit it as he made himself comfortable, hiding in skeins of smoke and haughty puffs with his nose held high.

His wife didn't answer, she began clearing the table, collecting crumbs, crumpled paper napkins, spoons and leftovers. He took his pencil and paper, and in a recently established evening ritual, began to draw.

"Last night I dreamed . . ." He stopped, suddenly realizing he could not tell her. In the background his sons were arguing. Laughter turned to cavalry charge, advance to silence. He heard nothing, not even noticing when they awkwardly entered and sat by the fire. They were fourteen and ten, the chessboard was shining, pieces threw flickering shadows; they played for themselves, the Great God of Chess, and in vain for his attention.

Deeper into winter saw him in much the same condition. He was healthy, quiet, perhaps he remained a little introverted, wrapped up in his work and family. Bandaged in memories selected from contrary filing systems. One drawer in for fantasy, another drawer out for reality. The sensation of living anew passed until he failed even to analyse his present. He woke – he worked – he ate – he slept.

On the sidelines of the ravaged weekend football pitch he watched his eldest son dribble a ball skilfully up the field towards the visiting team's goalmouth. He felt inclined to shout but didn't. He thought about games in earlier years: freezing mornings, watching the boys change into their shorts and shirts; sitting on frosty park benches struggling with numb fingers and stubborn bootlaces. In his pocket would have been a flask or quarter bottle of whisky, an alternative soul. At 9.30 in the morning he would already have been laughing and joking, his wit sparkling as ever, memories on tap. Nervous shyness would have fallen away, his true character emerging, blissfully nude. His mates would have stood close around him, for he'd been fun to be with, they might have thought him a loser, a potential suicide; but what a great man.

A shout from one of the players brought him sharply back to the present. It was ironic that now, when he was on a throne of overview, clear-sighted and even, they found him a bore. In the pub at lunchtime he always made them feel awkward, asking for mineral water while they warmed their sleeves of beer.

After all, it was only when drunk that he had excelled

himself in their eyes. Only when tipsily sailing with the
wind had he punched the local policeman, been with a
prostitute, sung like a Welshman, cried at the sunrise, wept
with emotion at being alive, or felt superhuman even with a
throat-croaking hangover.

"Well done lad/great play/sorry you lost/never mind/come
over here/get dressed/get warm."

The game over, he turned and looked towards the grey-
green hills. The sun was not high at this time of the year and
the sky was stunning, a mantle of cloud enveloping the scene
like a blanket, protecting the earth from the blind largess of
the sun. These hills sent him to his knees with a prayer only
eighteen months ago. Yet now he felt very little.

That evening at home in his chair by the fire he jotted
down new notes. He had some idea about a new way of
cooling glass, an idea the technicians at his company felt had
possibilities too. As he scribbled he remembered more fragments of pain: would he care if his best friend died? His
wife? His sons? Did he care about anyone?

There had been a girl. She entered his life under his
fingernail and prised it upwards until he screamed, while
sweetly shrugging off her charisma. Her general demeanour
suggested that she was just a girl, just another girl. His
memory of their meeting was vivid. He had gone to a nearby
town to visit a friend to go to a football match on a Saturday.
The game was to be one of the biggest he would ever see. It
was between the home team and the side who currently
topped the first division. The game was part of the League
Cup and his team had been in the semi-final.

He had suggested calling on the girl, to whom he had
merely taken a distant fancy; she had been like a challenging
whipped-cream and icing-bag job in a confectioner's window.
He had known of her involvement with one of his bosses,
but he had really seen her as she was. A drunkard had been
sobered. He had come to her as a newborn virgin boy; his
own mind blank, he had intended to woo blindly.

She responded succinctly to his arm's-length offer to the
game over the telephone: "I'd like to".

"You'd like to?" He felt he'd been disturbed from a dream within a dream. "I'll pick you up at 2.15 tomorrow – goodbye."

On the way to the game he and his friend stopped at a small house and knocked on the door. It was opened by the redhead, dressed ready for the game. The home-team colour around her pretty head. He had moved forward, shaken hands with her, and all three went off together to the game.

"I'm nervous," she said as they set off.

"Me too," he replied, but he felt like a conquering general walking over bodies. He had never felt so correct as with her by his side. He felt proud.

The game was a great success. They had drunk champagne on the terraces. The home team won. Everything seemed so distant, the cheers, the banners and colours flying, but "we" had won. Afterwards they went to a pub and drank more. The girl laughed at his jokes and seemed to fall for him. She drank more too, but didn't become slovenly or ridiculous. This pleased him, but somehow he himself got badly drunk. This was unusual for him; he felt control slip away. His vision became distorted and he found it hard to focus. His speech slurred under sporadic waves of nausea. He recalled her beautiful, laughing face leaning down to him as she picked him up by the lapels of his shirt.

"Behave," she commanded, "behave!" Playing up to it all, he pretended to fall down again and again while everyone laughed at his antics. He seemed to be toying with his audience, going through a charade of lushness behind which stood the seasoned, hardened drinker. Then there had been a darkness. What had he said in those last moments? What had he done? Why had he only awoken as they left the pub? Questions. Darkness. Pitch-black darkness.

His clearest memory was their return to the girl's house: they stood at her doorway. He and the girl were left to say their goodbyes. Feeling dizzy, he'd asked her if he could go in for a minute and sit down.

"You can't come in. I'm sorry but I'm in love with someone." The girl said this smilingly, without offence. In dream turning nightmare he had protested.

"I feel like hell, it's not for any other reason. I must come in. I can't go anywhere. Please let me come in, I'll just fall on the floor."

"Can't you get it into your thick skull? I love another man."

"Who is talking about love? Please, please. Let me in. I feel awful."

She kissed him and turned away smiling her goodnight. "Had a wonderful time, I promise, you were great fun. Goodbye."

The fire crackled and now (deep in reflection) he dug at it with a poker. His wife sat quietly knitting (his children long asleep) unaware of the parade in his mind.

Away from the doorway he had staggered and then fallen on the fish-slippery pavement. It had started to rain. The dark mining-town streets were empty and bleak. He'd fallen ungracefully on to his bottom. Humiliation, unmatched in his whole experience, overcame him. A pain grew in the pit of his chest. He had never felt like that before. He'd read about it, heard it sung in love songs, seen people who were suffering, talked to a brother who attempted suicide because of it, but had never felt it. This incredible pain was new to him. It seemed to be a living death that was somehow tied up with the battering of his ego and psyche, and yet he felt a definite physical pain, like being strangled from inside.

Just a girl. Just a girl. His broken heart was unfeeling, like shattered glass in an acid bath. He had had backed-up words like vomit in his throat. He'd sworn complaints. He'd cursed, kicked, wept, cried, and stubbornly clung on to what he was not. Fuck it! Fuck it! The words were pathetic.

He had laughed every now and then while struggling with the key to his own front door. Staggering in, he had slumped into the same chair he was now sitting on. Then he had wept.

He spent the following day (ironically, Valentine's Day) buying her flowers and trinkets, and a crate of the same champagne they had drunk on the terraces. Then before he visited her house again he wrote a letter:

I know this is insane, but I can't live without you. I hope to God this feeling will pass, because it is unbearable hell and bliss combined. I have never been so happy as when I was with you. I don't know you, I don't care about that, I measure only the moments. I am in agony now, please see me, please. I know you are in love with another man, I heard you, I remember, but in my dull misery I don't digest it – I refuse to. I love you, it's simple, unaccountable, and true.

His friend had delivered the letter. Then he telephoned her. She asked him not to make her feel so badly and wouldn't see him again under any circumstances. Blindly, he took his flowers and gifts to her house and knocked at the door, but there was no reply. He left the champagne and the roses on the doorstep. For a few minutes he slumped against the wall almost laughing at himself.

Suddenly he had heard voices from inside the house, and before he could stop himself, was banging on the door. The voices continued, but then he realized it had been only one voice – she was speaking into a telephone, crying, protesting. He turned and walked home. He knew she had been talking to the man she loved, the man he hated – no, not hated, he would forget it all.

As he remembered that day, the sensation of destitution and bereavement returned and he shifted uncomfortably in his chair, dropping his drawings. He closed his eyes and the memory of the pain brought tears. No one had ever felt that pain. No one.

He got up and looked at his wife. She caught him gazing at her.

"Are you all right?"

She stopped twitching the knitting needles in her hands. "Yes, love, I'm all right." She stood up, but he placed both his hands on her shoulders with firm affection and pushed her down again. He walked over to the dresser. He took out a bottle.

"No . . . no . . . not now. It's been so long." She had dropped her knitting into her lap and sat bolt upright. She felt rooted where he had pressed her into her chair. Her face was full of the fear that only she had fully experienced: fear of the fear to come.

It was only a matter of time now. She sat waiting for the meaningless toast, the glass-flourish.

He poured himself a large drink and returned to the chair, openly sobbing. He smiled at her through his tears and drank.

ROPES

It was Saturday night and I was in a disco for the workers of the hairdressing salons of the Edinburgh daylight. I knew nobody. All of them seemed to have no friends except the flashing trash-lamps and the eyeball-scouring lasers of the haphazard disco lightshow.

A group of people I obviously knew better than I knew, surrounded me, offering drinks; I felt fêted and among friendly people, if not among real friends. My real "friends" were resident at the other side of the club. It was too dark to see them clearly and I thought about the previous weekend when we had been in Glasgow and done all this before.

We'd dragged our clumsy entourage to a nightclub there. Like a busload of trippers we had literally tripped into the establishment, rather superior to the one in Edinburgh. Strange that Glaswegians with their reputation for toughness should offer a slicker, sleeker nightspot than the dilettantes of Edinburgh. At first glance the girls in Glasgow had seemed to be the most beautiful I had ever seen collected in one room. In particular, there were lots of faery blondes with ironed hair in ringlets. They remained unapproached. Oh, the price of beauty.

Rastus, at thirty-nine, looked weighty and febrile. His heavily pockmarked face and thin, tufted hair made him look corporeally viperous under the ultraviolet lights. Rastus is a man I have often been angry with, but his stamina and cheerfulness have made me love him. He was responsible for our lighting design on the stage, and much of the insanity of it. That night he danced like Martha Graham on the lavatory, his legs spread. He played an imaginary guitar and then, with two hands, wanked an imaginary four-foot long phallus. He had also hotly kissed and clutched at a girl I knew. Maggie had been collecting snapshots of us all, when someone had pulled her and a friend into our coach at the stage door of the show. This was a well tried method of romantic seduction. Once the door was closed and the coach driven away, all protestations seemed futile.

Suspicion grew. The two girls had talked very intimately into one another's ears. There was something deeper than friendship between them.

Rastus danced with her while yelling at me. "She's yours, you bastard. If you want her, she's yours."

He breathed over me and occasionally came closer and kissed me, forcing his tongue into my mouth as I stood to one side of the dance floor. The onlookers were confused but philosophical about Rastus's sexual preferences. "Well, you've earned it. You've bloody well earned it, I suppose."

Then he lunged at the girl again. She was dressed in denim jeans and jacket, her mid-blonde hair careless and her pretty face variously twelve then thirty years old in expressive response. I had taken a break from Rastus and Maggie, the crowded dance floor and the calm, staring Glaswegian crowd, and had joined Able, the man who tunes my guitars. He was celebrating his birthday that night. He'd found his "baby", as he called her, French, sophisticated and silent, loitering against a wall. He'd plied her with champagne and flattery, and defended her from his competitors with real valiance until, sneering apologetically, she'd slipped away. We'd all thought her a stuck-up bitch and had tried to cheer him up with her champagne, which he refused to drink. Able then left quite sadly, without a partner, and I went and found Maggie. She became very drunk and I guided her to my hotel room without difficulty. Her friend had remained under some table at the club.

I eased Maggie's ridiculous fur boots off, and pulled off her jeans and shirt. I had determined that she would rest, too perfect, too denigrated already. But she suddenly murmured her way through dreams into partial reality and slowly put her arms around my neck. In the half-light I looked down at her, she looked very young, but her breasts were very full. I slipped my hand behind her back and with one hand squeezed her brassière clasp open. I suddenly felt simian crouched over her and pulled myself back into shape. I flattened my back, broadened my shoulders, straightened my legs and thrust forward desperately, vainly fighting my own drunken impotence.

Later Rastus, his crazy friend Binky and possibly others, flailed at the room door yelling for us and anyone else they could use as an audience for the tail-end of their misty futility. The sun was gently rising by then. Maggie responded, her face covered in sweat. She opened her legs to the distant threat; this time we successfully coupled.

When I awoke after midday she was gone, and I cursed my incapacity to behave as the gentleman I'd so desperately wanted to be, or even as the paramour, both cavalier and tender. I had probably been snoring or crying in my sleep.

Now Maggie was here in Edinburgh, as were Rastus and co. Eastward ho! – debauchery, chapter two. Ray, my old writer friend, was along as an observer, to watch us act like animals so that he could spice up what would have to be a disgraceful biography of the band if it were ever to sell enough copies to make him rich. They were all there, the men who drove lorries, the lighting monkeys and riggers, the spot boys, the back-line crew and their tight-lipped molls. Sometimes all these hard-nuts danced; their black leather jackets and hard-worked denims incongruous in the glittering crowd, but they commanded love in my eyes. I was ever loyal reciprocally.

A young Scottish musician called Jock had also joined our ranks. He was in the early stages of his career, and constantly auditioning; he sang cavernously as though his chest was a copper tank. He sang us verses of his own songs, trying to rise above the noise of the music in the club. As a result, his melodies were lost on me. (Boys like this always have the most incredible nerve and staying power. They believe that simply being near someone who is successful enhances their own position, increasing their own chances of success.)

I reviewed the ménage, mustered in the dingy, dark corner like human-sized rats. Rastus had his phallus laid over a silver tray, and was making a girl shriek for mercy. She really did rather over-react, he was just a drunken exhibitionist with a very common appendage to display. Binky wore his Teddy-boy suit, with trousers cut for a midget; he had picked it up cheap at a tailor. The original client had wisely not returned to collect it. He was also wearing the 'lucky' green clown's shoes we thought might bring us successful shows. He was leaning against the disc jockey's rabbit hutch, a blood capsule crushed in his mouth. I kissed him sensually on the lips (to show I wasn't afraid of blood) and spent a sanguine night, looking as though I had been in a fight.

Some of the more sedate in our party, among them my driver Rex and secretary June, danced like the ageing Mods they were: one foot forward, other foot forward. They bounced up and down like pistons, slightly hunched over, arms pulling on non-existent ropes stretching out in front of them. It was tremendously endearing. The Baron, our manager, railed at one dancer after another, drawing on his massive vocabulary. He was too drunk to be entirely successful.

Rastus triumphed with his poetry, he always did. Rebuffed again by some gorgeous creature, he was in full tilt:

> You scum, you whore, you cur,
> who dare to slur,
> to cast at me a feeble fly,
> while I like salmon free do fly?

Surely Scotland had inspired him.

> You worm, who spurn a catch like me,
> well I can glance –
> not fly I see but flea.

This is about as close as I can get. His poetry didn't scan, but rhymed about every fourth word in a continuous cascade. Our evenings on tour were often spent in this familiar dread debauchery. We were the frayed rubber band inside the enormous balsawood airplane of rock and roll. Flying was a forgotten art.

Suddenly, through smoke and cyclops lamps, Able's baby from Glasgow reappeared. She called me over like a resident princess: "Why do you spend so much time with these garden gnomes?"

Her accent was steeply French. She said she was from Fontainebleau but as a child had lived on the island of Stornoway.

I was defensive; I have already explained my loyalties. "I like them, they are my friends."

"They are provincial. What do you read?"

"Conrad, Burgess, Bashevis-Singer, anything good – I'm still learning."

"Balzac." (This was a simple statement in space.)

"Of course," I lied, "all of Balzac."

"You are insecure away from your friends."

"Am I?" I did feel desperately insecure. I felt she had caught me out. "Perhaps I am, is that bad?"

"No, not always. I am insecure. Stay next to me. Look like you are talking to me."

I knew exactly what she meant, yet I thought I was appearing to talk to her already. I tried harder. I leaned against the wall and whispered nonsense into her ear. She threw back her head and laughed, even though I was not saying anything funny. She kept taking the cigarette from my lips to share it, never glancing around as I did. She drank my beer and enjoyed my hand on her waist. She was wearing what looked like a pair of nebulous silk pyjamas.

"Nice outfit." (What a wonderful line!)

"My mother gave it to me."

I was surprised because it was a sensuous affair, slashed at the front almost to the belt.

"I have to wear, on her instructions, this pin." She showed the nappy pin, just below her breasts, holding the blouse together.

I suddenly tired of amusing her. I decided to go back to my

rodent family. She followed this time, obviously not put off by the prospect of sitting with a large group of provincial garden gnomes. All the time, whoever I looked at or talked to, I thought of Maggie. I felt very cheap, playing 'appearance' games with this rather interesting girl I had once described as a stuck-up bitch while I looked over her shoulder with another girl on my mind. Layers upon layers of cheap night-club hypocrisy.

The evening went from mere asphyxia to total necrophilia, and the supposedly living finally retired to another venue.

In the hotel lobby a small assembly gathered that wanted to eat sandwiches and drink yet more alcohol. We started as a large group, but dwindled quite quickly to the hard-core, late-night stalwarts. As the sun came up there was Rastus, with a large and utterly charming porcine lady in a black dress. She laughed with careless vacancy at his anal persuasions. There was also Binky, who spent more time on prosopopoeia than denouement, but who nevertheless had us all in stitches. There was our young composer, Jock, who told us he was a Catholic and that his grandmother, hearing he was coming to see the band, said he should take some fish as it was Friday. There was the French girl, ever someone's 'baby', flicking her fingers for a room key, but laughing too, only really beautiful when she did so. We ate sandwiches, annoyed the early-rising guests, and laughed until tears streamed, at nothing and even less than nothing. The boredom was really quite exquisite.

As I sat in this brittle, overtired reverie I wondered if I could persuade Maggie to sleep with me there in Edinburgh. The previous night we had sat on the hotel stairs after the first show as the cleaners had mopped around our feet. I had been giving her a traditional line, I suppose, but it felt more significant than that at the time. She finally rebuffed me. We were in her home town; I thought that probably had a lot to do with her reticence. I found myself hoping that was why she refused me. Now, the moment was approaching when I should go up again to bed.

Without wishing anyone goodnight I got up and strolled quietly out of the hall into the lift and went up to my room. I was convinced that the French girl would follow me, probably demand my bed and insist that I sleep on the couch. I resolved to ignore her inevitable knocking at the door. I had developed a slight temperature during the day. It suddenly threatened nightmares and I became irrationally scared. Feverish and dangerously buoyant, I surveyed my room. The towel rail was thick chrome, twinkling like a New York Cadillac car bumper with flashing headlights. It was adorned with soft, white towels. The magnificent ancient sink supported two slowly dribbling taps. Looked at more closely, it was rust-stained beyond scouring, not fit to contain more than spittle. The monolithic mahogany wardrobe was partly open, the warm light of an electric fire setting the air aglow.

I heard noise in the sitting room adjacent to the bedroom in which I lay. I got up and walked in. In fever it looked like a sepulchre, vaulted and steaming. A large pillar dominated the centre of the room. I heard a voice calling my name. A woman in a black cowl came towards me and brought her face close to mine. For a second it was hard to tell if I was in a nightclub or a nightmare. I felt treacherous, I wanted to die. Her face, alternately the French girl's and Maggie's, was sexually alert. Her lips were moist and she caressed my swollen genitals.

"Look. Look what you have done."

She led me gently around the pillar, leading me by my cock. On the other side of the pillar was a gigantic cross, nailed to it suffered the Christ, his beautiful, racked face gazing down on me, tortured and forgiving.

"You caused this." The woman squeezed my hardened phallus, her voice and manner totally evil now.

"No! No. God forgive me – please forgive me."

I woke up wet and writhing as someone – I guessed it was the French girl – quit knocking at the door and went away. The final image of the dream was still burned into my retina – I had denied my Saviour and, after a brief reprieve,

37

left him in the torture chamber in which he faced his doom.

It was getting harder and harder to live with the truth; impossible to be honest because the truth was too awful. I was therefore ever a hypocrite, the punishment eternal and unbearable. It all seemed that serious to me at the time; Christ and girls and sleeping alone.

As I collected my baggage at the airport next day Ray came up to say goodbye.

"Why didn't you open the door last night?"

"I had a fever, nightmares. Anyway, I needed my bed, I wasn't about to give it up to that French bird."

"It was Maggie, she knocked for quite a long time, then gave up, she only wanted to say goodbye."

"I was young once," said the Baron.

"Yeah?" said Pete, "But you're still you. Every day you wake up and you are still you. It must be a great daily disappointment."

The Baron smiled. Any outsider could see that Pete was the star but the Baron was the boss. Between them at the bar sat a pretty, spicey girl.

"He's gorgeous," she said, nuzzling the older man, "I love you." The Baron grinned at this and kept his attention on Pete:

"I still wake up feeling sexy. I feel as sexy as I did when I was three years old." Pete and the pretty girl looked at him along the bar. "We were in some holiday camp in England, not long after the war. We stayed in a chalet. The mums and dads could go dancing while baby-sitters ran up and down checking the kids. I poured all my mother's perfume down the sink one night. I called to the nurse (she was kissing her boyfriend on a bench outside). She came in and I could feel her heat."

"At three years old?" sneered Pete.

"Yeah. I was super-bright even then. She picked me up and told me off. The place stank of gardenias. Then she put me to bed and kissed me. I fell in love with her. I had no idea who she was, or even what she was, but I remember feeling something erotic. She was there; my mother was out dancing."

"Poor thing," cooed the strawberry blonde.

"It explains a lot," said Pete, sinking his Guinness.

Back at the Baron's apartment they drank vodka. Pete sat next to the girl.

"You like music?" he asked her.

"Surely," she replied, sounding like a telephone operator.

"What kind of music?"

"Rod Stewart," she said, "My favourite is 'Tonight's the Night'."

"I've got some Irish folk music," said the Baron. "The Moving Hearts. I'll educate you." He moved quickly to the pile of cassette tapes.

"I've got my Rod Stewart right here," said the girl. "Put it on for me."

Crestfallen, the Baron acquiesced. The song wafted round the room. It was about a virgin girl getting her first lay. She was really lucky: her first lay was Rod. Pete sat there looking like he wasn't going to be able to stand it, but the song improved. He was checking her profile as she nodded wistfully to the rhythm; she was a very nice catch and he wasn't sure he would be able to achieve what Rod could achieve.

"Do you believe in reincarnation, Pete?"

"Yes. It makes some sense of life."

"Here's where she gets it!" she cut in, "he sings about her spreading her wings – you know what that means?"

"I think I get the picture."

The Baron was gazing into his vodka. Suddenly he got up. "I'm gonna turn in and read some Chandler."

"Don't go," cried the girl, "we want to hear your tape."

"Goodnight," said Pete. His manager turned around and went into the bedroom at the back shouting: " Stay if you like, spare bedroom's made up. 'Night."

The door closed. The girl looked at Pete and grinned. He placed her drink on the table and kissed her, feeling her body. After a few minutes' smooching around he stopped, lit cigarettes for each of them and gazed at her. They talked long and hard and Pete began to have difficulty keeping up with her flow of thought. She was sharp; uneducated but demanding and perceptive, quick to follow his stumbling reasoning. When he became exhausted she talked to him. He started to feel very unsettled. She was pretty. Every time he looked at her in the rosy light in the little sitting room he felt an old-time swoon.

Pete was a singer with a band. He hadn't had to fight to lay his hands on the girl. Some guy had made the mistake of bringing her into his dressing room after a show and he had impressed her. Six months later she appeared again, alone. Pete was an attractive guy, and he was talented, but he didn't really know that much about reincarnation. He bullshitted along, though, and the girl seemed eager to hear everything he had to say.

"Being a successful singer is like being a guru," he said. "Everyone wants to talk to you, be near you, love you."

"That's nice for you," she said, "really nice."

"It can be really hard too. Responsible. You know?"

"I need someone, Pete."

"Tonight's the night."

"No, Pete, I mean I need someone who can help me."

"I'm your man." Pete was being clumsy and he suddenly sensed it. "Listen, let me tell you about my boss, my chief. I've got a guru . . . this is him." Pete pulled out a picture of a man riding a little white donkey. The girl gazed at the picture and seemed transfixed.

"Take it," said Pete, "keep it, I've got another one with me."

Next morning the Baron was up first and his clattering woke them both. Pete looked at her and felt that swoon again. Her skin was so white, and she seemed so young.

"Ham and eggs, Okay?" shouted the Baron from the kitchen.

"Great," replied Pete, "and coffee?"

"Comin' up."

The girl jumped out of bed. Her body was delicate in the daylight. Pete looked as she brushed her hair. A few minutes later they were eating their breakfast. Pete was rehearsing, so he and his manager had to leave straight afterwards. They dropped the girl at her hotel.

"She's great, Pete. You in trouble?"

"Yes, I am." He was not smiling. He didn't crow like he usually did when he'd made a cheap conquest. "She's really great."

The car bounced over the San Francisco crossroads and

then wheeled into a little yard near the Chinese district. They got out and went in to the small rehearsal room. They were a little early, so they poured coffee from the beaker and sat on the tired, picked-at sofas.

"She told me her story; it's really weird."

"Yeah?"

"Her father was a very successful dentist. Really big man physically too. Her mother was a stunning English girl. She was a very pretty baby. At eleven years old she had a promising bosom and early periods. Her father ran off with his assistant nurse. Her mother moved her own lover in, a crazy stud of twenty-five who worked as an occasional logger in the hills. He lived off her."

"Asshole," said the Baron.

"You've heard nothing," said Pete, sipping from his plastic cup with shaking hands. "She fell in love with this guy."

"She was eleven?"

"What does that prove? You were saying yesterday you got the hots for a nurse when you were three."

"Not the hots exactly . . ."

"Listen, will you?" Pete spread his hands. "One night he crept into her room."

"What happened?"

"Nothing much at first. Then he started to go to her room a lot and finally brought her off one night without actually penetrating. She said that he was very big and they were both afraid, but he was careful with her."

"That was nice of him."

"She said he felt like a horse. She learned how to get him off. She would be completely drenched."

"I don't believe it. You're making it up."

"It's what she told me. She didn't cry. She didn't make any sort of big deal out of it. I don't know why, but I believed her. She said that eventually it had happened properly."

"Tonight's the night," sang the Baron tunelessly.

"Yeah. But the next night was another night."

"What happened the next night?"

"The woodcutter kidnapped her."

"What?"

"He took her up to his cabin in the Sierras."

"How old was she then?"

"She was just twelve years old. They had been building up to her first time for a few months and did it on her birthday."

"What about her mother?"

"Her mother did nothing."

"Nothing?" The Baron screeched in a whisper. "Didn't she call the police?"

"Nope."

"Shit."

"They lived there for three years in total isolation," continued Pete. His manager sat open-mouthed, not knowing what to believe. "He brought her books and food, and the rest of the time they just kept at it. She hated her mother for not coming to find her, but she hated her more for having loved the logger before she did and for losing her father too."

The Baron thought about the girl as Pete lit a cigarette. He couldn't believe the story. She was an innocent, fragrant girl. It couldn't be true.

"What was it like with her?" he asked.

"She was good, very good, she has a wonderful body but . . ."

"What?"

"She was really big, you know, down there. Enormous. It embarrassed me."

"Why? Did you feel small?"

"Of course I felt small, you toe-rag. But it was the noise we made, she was big and wet. I can't spell it out, she's a sweet lady but . . ."

"Okay, so she was big. Go on."

"When she was fifteen he took her back."

"To the mother?"

"Yeah."

"Jeez. I bet the old lady went crazy."

"She did nothing. She took the logger back and her daughter went up to her room and resumed listening to them making love at night. The police had listed her missing, but when they heard from her father, who told them she'd been found again, everyone was happy. She couldn't work out why no one was making any kind of fuss. Neither her mother nor father mentioned anything. She was grown up, seasoned and mature. Last time either of her parents had seen her she'd been a little girl."

"What did she do, Pete? Go crazy?"

"No, she went to work for the father as a dental assistant. His girl had left him. She kept living with her mother and the logger. The logger never touched her again and none of them ever mentioned it."

"Three years in a cabin. With a logger," said the Baron.

"Three years in a cabin with her," corrected Pete.

Pete had nearly wept when he and the girl were parted the next night. He was off to Reno and she went back to Southern California where her father had his practice and her "family" were. She wore a rose in her hair. She said she would prefer to see him with a beard when they met again. "And an axe?" he thought.

Five years had passed and Pete grew older. His luck stayed in for a long time. He never met the girl again, or anyone like her, but he and his manager did the circuit and made a good living. One Christmastime Pete's liver finally gave out. He was trying to give up the booze, taking all kinds of pills and vomiting a lot, seeing little stars and using sleepers to keep himself from being bored. With a bottle he was alone, without it he was catatonically fucked up. The Baron kept an eye on him. He telephoned as usual one night: he had a special message.

"That crazy bint from Southern Cal just called the office, Pete. She wanted to talk to you. She wanted your number. She sounded very weird. She didn't really remember me. I told her that I couldn't give her your number."

"It's okay," Pete was trying not to retch, "give me the number. I'll call her from here." The Baron gave him the number and left him to make his call.

Pete sat down and thought about the girl. She was pretty. It was all he could remember really. He dialled and she came on the phone.

"Pete! Oh, Pete, thank God!"

"What's up? How are you?"

"Pete, I'm in trouble." She sounded so familiar. "You still got your guru?"

"I still have a picture or two, yeah." Pete was mystified.

"I got a guru, Pete. Not like yours exactly, but a bit like him. When you left me in Frisco I was really sad."

He laughed bitterly: "I'm married to my work."

The girl carried on, ignoring him: "I met this guy in LA. He had a kind of ashram. I joined it. I wanted to be a part of something good. A family. We were all friends. We helped one another. It was great, Pete. It was all thanks to you."

"Well, that's wonderful . . ."

"Mmmm, wonderful," she agreed.

"Where do you meet?"

"We don't meet any more. The guru went to Houston. He got into Jesus. He has a TV show, pay as you pray, y'know?"

"Yeah," said Pete. "What happened to his followers?"

"He keeps in touch with us by a kind of telepathic contact."

"Oh yeah?"

"With me, he keeps very close. I am in this house and he visits me here. I can't leave."

"He keeps you there against your will?"

"Well, not exactly, but I can't leave. He would miss me when he visited me."

"How can he visit you, if he lives in Houston?"

"He comes in the guise of a little boy, from down the street."

"A what? I feel like I should come and see you straight away. You're in trouble."

"Would you?" she asked, with a great sigh of relief, "That would be incredible. You know about all these things, don't you? When could you come?"

"Well, I would have to work out some flights . . ."

The girl interrupted him suddenly: "He's back, he's here. I'll have to go."

"Who's back?" shouted Pete. Down the other end of the line she was babbling at someone in the background.

"My guru. Sorry, have to go . . ." The line went dead and Pete shoved the receiver down.

He wasn't going to Southern Cal; he could hardly get out of bed. He was weak and he was sick. But the girl had worried him; he wanted to help. He called a friend of his near her. The guy was a psychotherapy student. He would be able to help her. Pete went to bed, forgot all about it and slept well for the first time for a month.

Next day he woke up blearily. The Baron stood over him.

"What are you doing here?"

"Get up, Pete, I got some news." The manager was cool. Pete got up, took a trip to the bathroom and joined the Baron in the kitchen of the large apartment on Nob Hill.

"What's up?"

"I got a call from your friend in South Cal."

"The girl?"

"No, the guy you sent to her. He tried to call you direct. Those pills make you dead, Pete. Be careful."

"Yeah. What happened?"

"She's in a home, man."

"What?" Pete leaped up.

"She's accused of kidnapping some twelve-year-old boy. She's been doing bad things to the kid."

Pete finally got himself straight about a year later. He quit the booze, quit the casinos, and the Baron went home to England. Pete decided to close the Nob Hill apartment and put it up for sale. Clearing it up he came across a magazine full of naked people. He was about to throw it into the trash when he recognized her face. She was with a very big man. She was holding him in one hand, and her little Cindy doll in the other. The photograph had been taken in a dentist's chair.

FISH SHOP

This giant of a man threw the full weight of his body against mine. He was standing in the audience, on a chair behind me, and he put his arms around my neck to support himself. He smelt like a rag used to wipe beer splashes from a bar. He was wet with sweat, and his arms were strong and irresistible. His hands were like the spreading branches of a small, hardy shrub reaching out to the sun, sinuous and brown in the theatre lights.

Performing with his band on the stage was my friend Pete, a narrow man with eyes like the eyes a child sees when it stands on its head and looks into a mirror. He was swinging his guitar like a battle-axe, slicing a microphone stand in two and sending the tragic instrument hurtling across the stage, its cable curling.

The giant clasped me tighter as he screamed his approval. I had become his stilts. He fell forward as I collapsed under his shaking, writhing weight. He crashed to the ground in front of me, swinging a vain punch at me while he laughed and spluttered, and I laughed too. I recognized him from the distant past without recalling exactly who he was.

Backstage I told Pete I would not risk seeing his band play again; the audience was too wild and ebullient; I always felt too close to the edge. Another friend of his had laughed at this and playfully punched at his face. Pete passed a weary hand over his lip and checked the tiny blood trickle. Laughing too, he winced back at his antagonist. He did not return the punch, and the two never spoke.

A few weeks after the concert I interviewed him for a newspaper. We decided it would be grand to walk slowly through our old home town. We could see the small church halls in which he had first performed; we'd walk past the little terraced houses of young girls with whom he had fallen in love; we might visit his school and then walk past his parents' house. This was not for nostalgic reasons; we had covered the nostalgia a thousand times before. We hoped we might unearth overlooked fragments of memory.

We stood in the sad street where his old junior school still was: a Victorian testimony to England amid high-rise blocks.

"What the hell do they think the kids are going to do? Escape?" Pete spat against the flaking paint of the proud school railings that stood almost double our height, like prison bars.

"None of this was here when we came to school." He gestured at the tower blocks, "Just rows and rows of little terraced working men's houses, two up, two down. It sounds so bloody clichéd now of course. Now these poor bastards live thirty up and thirty down, with the lifts blown in piss and spray paint."

"Don't get maudlin, Pete. You came from here, some other great bands came from here. It's always from places like this that good new stuff emerges."

Pete cut me short. "Sorry." He grabbed my shoulder with one arm. I felt a second of unfamiliar warmth, a privileged closeness. It was like hiding under a general's coat as snow starts to fall before an advance. I suspected an ulterior motive.

We walked past the school buildings that were already lost in time in this decaying estate, and headed towards the rather more substantial area Pete had once lived in himself.

"So – you'll never come to see us play again? Too rough for you?"

"Well – I don't know. I did get my neck severely bent when you were throwing your guitar around. You were knocked about in the dressing room yourself. Who was that guy? Why didn't you say anything to him?"

"An old adversary. No – an old friend really, we're old buddies."

"Great way to greet an old buddy: crack his lip."

"Don't worry about me."

"I won't, Pete, I promise."

His attitude often infuriated me. He was no street fighter and never had been. Yet he expected any journalist who approached him professionally to act as though he was.

In reality he was thin, exceptionally frail; not tall, but gauntly attractive with dark hair never left long. He always wore considered clothing, with lazy respect for fashions. He drew people to him, but his true motives were never totally clear. I knew him better than most. I knew the man who hid below the surface. He had learned as an awkward young man how to use people to get what he wanted.

Later, the grey darkness I remembered descended on Acton. The streets took on their familiar negative glow. The pavements tried to hide, the streetlamps tried to fade, the front doors of homes full of people shouted, "Nobody home! No one lives here!"

Pete and I had grown up together, although we had attended different schools. As a fifteen-year-old Pete discovered that the old Spaniard running our local fish-and-chip shop had been a famous guitarist back in Spain. Pete was a flamenco fan and had recognized the man's name, Jacob Grajera, on an old record he found in a junk shop. He used to go and annoy the old boy, trying to get him to admit he had once been famous. Pete wanted some lessons.

Jaco was a striking figure, fairly short, but with deep black hair and a fine moustache. He was about sixty with a warm face and manner. His hands were particularly fluid and expressive; he did even simple things like shovelling chips into paper envelopes with a grace that displayed a perfect balance of masculine and feminine. His eyes sparkled with wit and mischief. He didn't have a wife and some of us thought he might be homosexual. But if he was, he was discreet.

Jaco's fish shop was magnificent. It was full of highly polished opaque glass. Light green and pink. It was a traditional shop with marble walls and floors, massive stainless-steel fryers and huge jars of pickle and gherkins on the counter.

One day Pete got Jaco to admit to his glorious past, and one evening arranged to take his guitar to the shop after it had closed and let the old guy show him some flamenco licks. At first Pete used flattery to appeal to Jaco's vanity; the old man had been neglected for a long time. But Pete was a true musician whom Jaco realized was genuinely inspired and interested to learn. They began to work together regularly, often playing into the early hours. Naturally the rumour spread among Pete's friends that he was paying for his flamenco lessons with sexual favours. He never denied the story.

One day when Pete was going to a group rehearsal he saw Bonzo, his fellow misfit and old school friend, talking with a pretty girl of about fourteen.

Pete was attracted to the girl, who was holding her baby sister. (There is usually one girl like this on every street: a natural star in her own modest element.) In that area of Acton there was no other girl with the same sparkle. Many of her less pretty friends grew up to be more accomplished, and to have handsomer and more successful husbands with nicer houses and healthier children, but at that precise moment she reigned supreme.

She wasn't resented by her peers, but she could be rather sullen; she knew she didn't have to work very hard to get attention. She was devoted to her little sister, but the fact that they were such constant companions indicated that all was not well at home. She seemed, from a distance, a very friendly and well balanced girl.

Pete was amazed that she should waste her time with such an ugly boy. (Bonzo had a pointed head, which only a skilful haircut could hide. His schoolboy crop didn't flatter him.) Pete laboured under the misapprehension that every female in the world was as prejudiced as his mother, who hated ugly men. Bonzo was one of the friends he dared not take home to meet his family. Pete knew his mother would disapprove.

Pete stayed at the corner watching the little group laughing together. Bonzo spotted him and ran over.

"Wotcha, Pete. Going to rehearse?"

"Waiting for the van."

"Playing the White Hart again?"

"Every Wednesday now."

"Cor, you got it sorted." Bonzo was impressed.

"Who's that bird?" asked Pete, gesturing to the girl.

"My cousin Fiona. Right little goer. Lives opposite us."

"She's great-looking," said Pete. "You sure she's related?"

"Don't come it, you cunt. She lets me do it."

Bonzo was hurt. He flattened a soft-drink can lying in the gutter into a wafer under his heel.

"I don't believe it," said Pete.

"I'm not a leper," retorted Bonzo, "I get it between her legs – she loves it."

Pete looked over at the girl as she swung her little sister around. In the late afternoon light she was especially pretty. Her blonde hair in a ponytail and her green check school dress somehow refuted Bonzo's story. Pete pulled his guitar case upright and hugged it tightly as he saw the group's van in the distance. Bonzo ran back without another word. The van pulled up, its sliding door rolled back and Pete jumped into the space behind the driving seat.

The van careered down the street. Chris, the band leader, showed Pete the trophies from the previous night: soiled underwear and empty beer bottles. The older band members were trying to persuade Pete to join them one evening for a night with the girls after a show. Pete thought they were all a bit coarse. He gazed out of the window as they passed the large supermarket in the middle of town. As usual, the Parrish boys were leaning against the railing at the kerb. It was hard to believe the two men were brothers. One had blonde hair, the other black. But they were both short and stocky and had more in common: they were both keen on cheerful violence. They scowled impressively at the passing traffic. Ronny, the older one, was laughing with his pretty girlfriend. Vic, the dark younger brother, was sullen. Usually they were friendly to Pete, but he'd heard terrible stories about them.

Later that night the band played at the White Hart. Chris and Pete went for a drink in the interval. While they were at the bar Ronny praised the band. Vic nodded his agreement. Pete felt uncomfortable.

"Vic wants you to play at his wedding," said Ronny.

"Congratulations, Vic," stuttered Pete. "We will of course."

"We can afford to pay," said Vic knowingly. Just then, Bonzo walked into the bar. Pete felt himself greatly relieved to see someone of his own age.

"Come to see us play, Bonzo?"

"No, not really." Suddenly he appeared harder and older. Pete realized he was going to get no comfort from his friend and, looking at his watch, skulked out into the street.

He looked over to Grajera's fish-and-chip shop which was right opposite. He thought again about Bonzo making clumsy love to Fiona. In the pub with the villainous Parrish boys, Bonzo had almost seemed like one of them. Suddenly he actually saw Fiona, dragging her little sister along on the other side of the street. He crossed to intercept her. She went into the chip shop and Pete arrived in time to hear her order. Jaco started to organize her food.

"Ah, Pete . . . I hear your band tonight, it's good. My evening is complete now. Beautiful music and beautiful girls."

Pete was embarrassed, but Fiona took no notice at all, slapping her young sister's hand down from the counter.

"Bonzo is over the Hart," Pete told the girl.

"Chasin' the Parrish boys, I s'pose," she sneered.

"Yeah. They're there. You're his cousin, aren't you?"

"Cousin? Me?" The girl looked quite insulted. Pete said nothing more.

Jaco gave the girl her fish and chips and she left. He turned to Pete. "For you?"

"Nothing, thanks. See you later." He turned and followed

the girl outside. He gazed up the street after her. He felt
Jaco's eyes on the back of his neck.

The next day in the local park, mothers were pushing their
babies in prams while a few older folk walked their dogs.
The weather was British and gloomy. Pete and Bonzo were
slouching along talking, kicking their way through the untidy
grass.

"Whatd' you mean, she isn't my cousin?"

"Don't jump down my throat, Bonz. I saw her last night in
Jaco's and she just said she wasn't your cousin, in a toffee-
nosed way, that's all."

"Hanging around Jaco's again? Got something for you has
he?"

"Watch it, Bonzo, or I'll flatten you!" Pete said angrily.

But Bonzo turned on him suddenly and knocked him to
the ground with a hard punch to the shoulder. Then he held
him down. Pete's nose started to bleed in the scuffle.

"Leave it out, I'm getting blood all over my stage trousers."

"Thought you were gonna flatten me? Think I'm a bloody
idiot? Think I can't pull Fiona? Well, listen to me. I ain't
'Bonzo' any more, to you or anyone else. Understand? I'm
Brian. That's my name. Brian, BRIAN, BRIAN." Bonzo punched
the name into Pete's chest. Suddenly he stopped and let Pete
get up.

"I might have a pointed head, but I get to feel Fiona's tits . . .
and a lot more, wop-lover."

Pete was still very shaken. He followed as Bonzo moved
slowly across the park, kicking angrily at scraps of paper,
waiting for his temper to subside.

"Listen," Pete said stiffly, "I'm sorry. Fiona seemed worried
about you hanging about with the Parrish boys. She probably
just meant she didn't feel you were the cousin she used to
know. You're growing up, getting harder maybe?"

Bonzo softened. "We did a factory last night after the
Hart," he said proudly. "I got twenty quid in cash just for
standing outside."

"What did you do?" Pete was incredulous.

"We took the whole bleeding safe. There were eight of us and we lifted it into your van."

"Our bandwagon?"

"Didn't Chris tell you?"

"No, he didn't. Listen, Brian, you be careful. The Parrish boys are on a downhill run, you know that. They're sure to end up inside. I'm amazed Chris is still playing games like that when he can earn a living with the band."

"Exactly," retorted Bonzo. "You and him can make a living playing in your sodding band. But I can't. I can't play nothing. Everyone has treated me like an idiot, and for years I've been smashed around at school. Well it ain't going on. I'm doing boxing on Mondays and I can already do twenty press-ups and I ain't scared of getting blood on my clothes."

Bonzo brushed himself off and walked away across the park.

Pete and Bonzo both had to deal with their anger. They were both misfits, but Pete had found a way of utilizing his frustration in his music. Bonzo had nothing but his ability to develop muscles and drink himself some bravado; and Fiona – he had her. Pete found himself cursing the guitar he had chosen as a channel for his youthful energies. His friend had played it straight down the middle, faced his inadequacies and, ironically, got the girl.

In the back room of Jaco's shop the sound of fiery flamenco guitars filled the air. Jaco stamped while Pete played chords. Then Jaco picked rapid staccato melodies over the vamping, his long, lean fingers curving gracefully on to the strings, delicate and yet immensely powerful.

Jaco watched Pete playing. He saw the vengeance in the young man's eyes. He recognized in Pete his own frustrated, insular passion. It made him feel sad. Later he talked about his own youth. He had loved a girl who had looked a little like Fiona but darker, of course. Jaco wooed her with his guitar, night after night, often suffering beatings from her father and her brothers who disapproved of him. He himself would fight off rival boys in the little Castilian village where they lived. But it was his guitar playing that won her heart.

He often played at bullfight parties thrown by successful matadors. His girlfriend would dance seductively. The bullfighters, used to getting any women they flirted with, had to laugh when she rushed to Jaco's side. Eventually Jaco and his girl were married, but within a short time the Civil War broke out in the south and Jaco went to fight and to entertain his compatriots. When he got back after the fighting she had gone, had left to live with a wealthy stock-breeder. In the little village the shame was too great to bear.

He smashed his guitar at the doorstep of their little house. He even destroyed the case.

"You came over here?" asked Pete. "You ran away?"

"Yes. Here, I don't have to think about her, or the fighting."

Somehow Jaco's story gave Pete the courage he needed. The next day he bought some flowers and went to visit Fiona at her home. She sat him down in her front room, but as he tried to get his guitar from its case she closed the lid. Then she stood up and slipped out of her dress.

Vic Parrish's wedding was a typically working-class affair, but it was held in a large garden in a well-to-do district. (Vic's new wife had an enterprising father.) The next door fence had been carefully taken down to make more space, and a stage had been built near the house. It seemed as though half the neighbourhood had turned up.

The Parrish boys' family was a surprisingly conservative collection. Their father was a sturdy, red-faced man with thick curly hair, and their mother a small gentle woman with tiny eyes. They were both smiling and neatly dressed. The uncles and aunts, cousins and friends stood around in self-conscious groups. They fingered their buttonholes and nervously knocked back their glasses of champagne. A few younger couples danced to Pete's band in the sunshine while children peeped over the fence to enjoy the festivities.

On the stage Pete felt irritated as he watched Bonzo talking intimately to Fiona. She was obviously a little drunk and was flirting with him. When Bonzo turned away from her and went over to an older, brassier girl, she was clearly put out.

Before Pete could dwell on it too much Chris announced: "We continue with a song written in honour of the bridegroom by Pete, our little resident genius."

The band began the song and Pete sang venomously. The words celebrated men being real men; real men didn't need to display their toughness but needed to be able to know compassion and self sacrifice. Pete hadn't written the song for Vic Parrish at all, but for Jaco. Chris knew that. Pete blanched when he spotted Jaco standing quietly at the french windows near the house, a drink in his hand.

When the song was over the whole audience and the neighbours cheered. Everyone spontaneously sang, "For he's a jolly good fellow", slapping Vic on the back and toasting him and his wife, with their glasses held high. Pete jumped down and stood, shaking visibly, at the side of the stage.

"What's wrong with you?" shouted Chris. "That's supposed to be a happy song."

"Nothing wrong with the song, just the bleeding dedication."

"Ease up, Pete, they're paying us a one-er."

Chris went back to the band shaking his head and they all relaxed, waiting for Pete to recover. The crowd sang noisily.

Bonzo sneaked up on Pete and whispered into his ear, "That was a nice tune. Wrote it for Vic, did you? Thought you disapproved of villains."

"Look, Brian, lay off." Pete was angry but knew he had to contain himself; Bonzo was drunk and looked dangerous, and Pete had to get back up and play.

"I used to like you, Brian. I never pushed you around. We were mates . . ."

Before he could finish, his rival grabbed him by the collar and pulled their noses together. "Keep away from my cousin, you bastard!"

"She's not your cousin. You're doing all right with that big blonde, aren't you? Stick to your own sort, Brian. Leave me and Fiona alone." Pete was losing control.

Bonzo pushed him. "Can't let my cousin associate with a wop-wanker."

At this taunt Pete saw only whiteness before his eyes. Without thinking he started shouting at Bonzo at the top of his voice: "Jaco's a bloody better man than any of the small-time villains here. He's tougher and brighter and he's been through hell and his music shows it . . . I wrote that song for him, not your bloody precious Vic." Bonzo let Pete gush. The crowd fell silent and everyone clearly heard this last remark. Pete grabbed his guitar and pushed out through the crowd. Vic Parrish looked uncomfortable as his new bride teased him.

"A man is man . . .," she sang with a cackling laugh, echoing the chorus of Pete's song.

Pete arranged to take Jaco and Fiona for a picnic later that week. They went to Virginia Water and sat in the sunshine. Jaco and Pete played their guitars and at one point Jaco managed to get Fiona to dance with him flamenco-style. She laughed as they stalked each other in a circle. It was an appealing scene. Jaco was not portly, and (for his age) his hair was still thick. He pulled himself up straight, threw back his head and clapped his hands as Pete strummed dramatically. Fiona took the hem of her skirt in both hands and swished it from side to side, revealing her pretty legs and frilly petticoat.

Pete and Fiona saw one another nearly every day for the rest of the week. He had forgotten about the wedding and had left the band. He was finding Fiona demanding. He couldn't ever seem to satisfy her. In the weekday summer afternoons they would often make love in his parents' bed. Fiona would actually weep in frustration when he fell asleep after reaching his own climax. Fiona didn't talk of marriage to Pete. She felt it was far too early. Anyway she was keeping half an eye on Brian. He was getting more attractive as he acquired confidence. All she had to do was decide which of the young men would make her pregnant.

Apart from feeling a little outclassed sexually by Fiona, Pete was afraid she was too shallow to be his companion for life. He was already wondering if she was the kind of woman he wanted on his arm when he entered fashionable restaurants in the future of his fantasies.

One evening as Pete walked Fiona home they passed Ronny and Vic Parrish leaning against a wall with Bonzo. Pete was fearful for a second but relaxed when they smiled and nodded. They were all eating chips. Bonzo offered Fiona a sample as they passed. She smiled shyly but refused. When they were out of earshot she said: "I'm fed up with bleeding chips."

"Right, listen, we'll just pop in and say goodnight to Jaco then go over the Wimpy." Pete was quite chirpy.

"Do we have to go and see Jaco?" whined Fiona.

"What's the matter?"

"He gives me the willies – the way he looks at me – it gives me the willies." She shuddered and snuggled up to Pete's arm as they walked.

"But Jaco's great, and he really likes you . . . come on."

But Fiona was not going to be persuaded. She dropped Pete's arm and stopped a few yards from the entrance to the shop. The bright pink-green light shining out through the steamy window illuminated the late-night mist. Her face was so beautiful in the glow. Her petulant Cockney pout and her shining hair under a headscarf were simple elements that set Pete's heart beating. She was making him choose. Why?

Suddenly Jaco was at the door of the chip shop. Fiona looked at him and scowled. Then she looked at Pete expectantly. But he wasn't quick enough. She lost patience, and with a little stamp of her foot walked back towards Bonzo and the Parrish boys in the distance.

Utterly confused and still slightly shocked, Pete wandered into the shop.

"No Fiona?" asked Jaco.

"She'll be all right. Just give me a couple of bags of chips and I'll follow her." He slapped the money on the counter top.

Jaco gazed over his shoulder out into the street. "Go after her now, Pete. Go on, go." He was emphatic.

"What about the chips?"

Jaco seemed to lose his temper. "Go now, Pete. Go on, GET OUT."

Pete was scared and backed out of the shop. His mind was full of images. Jaco and Fiona dancing on the grass at Virginia Water. Bonzo insinuating that he and Jaco were lovers. He saw Jaco fighting off his rivals as a young man. Was Jaco angry Pete had let Fiona go? Did he only want her, not him any more? Suddenly his mind cleared as someone pushed him aside. As he gazed with horror back into the shop through the great shining window, he saw Bonzo cutting wildly at Jaco with a long knife. Vic and Ronny smashed at the beautiful glass and marble with pickaxe handles. Pete couldn't move. All he could think was that Fiona had known it was going to happen.

Then suddenly, as though in a dream, time seemed to slow down completely. The window of the shop clouded over with condensation. He would remember the scene for ever. He would celebrate it and mentally re-run it again and again so he would never forget it. It was a glorious sight, an incredible explosion. The still shafts of light hanging in the gentle evening mist quivered as the first blast of icy condensation frosted the shop window in an even sheet. The light in the street dimmed visibly. This had the effect of making the open doorway relatively brighter and more nightmarish. The traditional sunrise pattern of the window was barely visible until streaks of hot fat began to clear the view again. Jaco, sheltering under the counter, had dropped a bucket of cold water into the biggest vat of boiling fat, sending it gushing to the ceiling in a fountain.

In the doorway, the air itself turned gold. Jewel-like drops of oil showered down in steaming vapour trails. Almost as soon as the window had misted up, a great blast of steam wafted into the street. Pete felt like the witness to some awesome, nuclear test of devastating power.

The fat was now dripping slowly down all over the three young thugs: they screamed and slid on the marble floor trying to escape. They all rushed past Pete who was still standing numbly a few yards from the doorway. Pete looked as Bonzo, holding his badly burned arm, ran up the street. He saw Fiona stop him under the street lamp. She had waited. They looked back at Pete for a second, then hurried together away into the night.

Pete gazed dumbly at the now silent scene, not daring to move. The window was slowly clearing. As it did he saw Jaco behind the fryer, picking up scattered chips with his fingers and putting them into a paper bag. Then Jaco walked from the shop. As he offered the pathetic little parcel of chips, Pete could see Jaco's arm was bleeding where Bonzo had cut him.

"Just one packet now, eh, Pete?"

Now Pete and I walked past the old fish shop. It was being run by a Chinese family.

Pete says that night was important to him. The event seemed to be symbolic: the moment when he finally decided to break away from the little town and the people that he had grown up with.

Maybe his past went up with the boiling fat that night, but his anger remained. The wrong person chose to become his ally. He had wanted the young girl, but he got the old man, and he wasn't sure he really trusted Jaco's motives.

Pete had nevertheless made his allegiance plain from the beginning; he'd picked his winner in Jaco and paid the price. As we looked at the shop where the incident had happened years before, he fingered the recent cut on his lip.

PANCHO AND THE BARON

I

And what did I do?
What a boring question!
At first I did little
Except thunderous drumming
I hated his cynicism
Was afraid of his keenness
His sharp perspicacity
His need to be leader
And so I co-operated
Became his adversary
Distracted his suitors
Conquered his conquests
Then I partly surrendered
I applauded his ability
Enjoyed his laughter
As I used him as a straight man
Decorated his inventions
Tampered with his master plan
Pretended he was invidious
And then I submitted
Admitted I loved him
And dared to display this
What did I do?
Only what any brother would have done.

II

When I first heard that Pancho had died all I could think of
was that I had survived. I had outlasted him. In a sense, I had
won.

He had been an incredible man, a brilliant musician, also a
violently inspired social showman. He often felt like a brother
to me. But he had occasionally terrified me, and I was
relieved he would threaten me no longer.

Three years later, in my seedy hotel room in New York, I sat with Able and we talked about the old days. I kept saying over and over again: "I survived". I was about two weeks into a desperate recording session in a small studio there. As a professional drunk I was a great success with the New York musical élite, and I had been entertaining people night after night in my room, at restaurants and nightclubs.

One night a girl visited with a boyfriend, and the three of us were left at the break of day talking about our troubles. When they both got up to leave, the traffic already noisy in the street, the girl tried to steal my scarf, I don't know why. I was full of brandy, but I spotted the scarf and pulled it from her neck.

"Stay," I said.

"I can't," she replied, "he'll be upset."

She went, but she called me the next day and I arranged to see her. She worked for a big American clothes designer. She was his assistant. She wore glasses and was very beautiful and I'm certain enjoyed many passes. I hope she enjoyed mine.

"You're a really nice guy," she said as I came into her. She was lying face down and I had made all kinds of noise. I didn't stop to think that she might be taking the rise out of me. I got up after a long period of respectful afterglow; someone was knocking at the door.

"Who is it?"

"It's Spud."

"Hold on." I put on a robe and went into the lobby. The girl went into the bathroom. I opened the main door.

"Can I come in?" asked Spud. "I'm afraid I've got some bad news."

"Yeah, sure. What's up?"

"The Baron's dead. He died yesterday. Fell down some stairs. Got beaten up apparently."

"Shit."

That was my last word on the subject for about half an hour. The girl came out and I explained I was having some problems. She took it very well and left. She probably thought I was giving her the usual bullshit. Who's to say she wouldn't have got the usual bullshit? She was a very pretty girl. When I called her later she was out and didn't return my messages.

"Spud," I said after a long silence, "what am I doing?" He didn't reply, but just looked at me. He sat with his loose, expressive hands on his knees. His gestures seemed to be writing me off with no visible movement. I got up and looked out over Central Park.

"I've survived." That was all I could think of to say before I went to the studio and finished work on another song. "First Pancho, now the Baron."

Later that day Spud, Able and I went out to a nightclub and saw some New York musicians having a good time. When we got back to the hotel I was accompanied by a girl who looked very much like the girl I had slept with on the previous night. As she thrashed about all over the bed I started to weep a little.

"What's the matter?" Her face was sincere.

I couldn't think of any reply to the question. I'd survived again and I wasn't even trying. I composed myself, smiled weakly at the girl and nobly finished what I'd started.

III

And I?
I challenged him
Seduced him from the bosom
Drew him from the sycophants
Fought off the leeches
Recognized his greatness
Flattered youth's ego
Overrated his vitality
Ignored his flatulence
Resisted his attraction
Listened to his babbling
Acknowledged his genius

Lived with his impudence
Struggled with his naïveté
Compared him to no one
Trained him to prosper
Urged him to aspire
Forced him to deliver
Drove him to achievement
Praised his independence
I was his mentor
I was his manager
What did I do for him?
Only what any father would have done.

I always seem to be in New York on the anniversary of Lennon's death. That happened in December 1980. On the first anniversary I was invited to the home of a big music entrepreneur in the city. There were several notable people there. We were all trying to pretend we could rise above our emotions and feelings of complicity. (Everyone in the music business felt responsible for what had happened.)

The apocryphal stories rolled out. Someone said that they had seen Lennon recording his last album.

"How was he?" I asked.

"He was happy, but strange as ever."

"How do you mean?"

"Not saying very much. Keeping himself to himself."

Oh, the tight friendships, the shared secrets, the unique and privileged intimacies between a star and his so-called friends. It is selfish in a peculiar way. Selfish of the star for deviously manipulating his acquaintances with glimpses of his "real" self; of the friends who, by vague innuendo, insinuate unprintable facts.

The party was suddenly disrupted by the arrival of an old friend of mine from England, Van Smith-Hartley. He was raging drunk. We were prepared to forgive him – he had lost his band only a year or two before – but his outburst startled everyone.

"We've brought our children up to sit with glued-on headphones while they scribble away at their homework, music throbbing in their mental genitals. They confuse sex with aspiration, violence with fortitude.

"They scramble the innate rhythmic response granted man by a generous God, with getting high in smoke-filled discos, or throwing Coke cans and firecrackers at stadium concerts. They analyse the words of songs that might just as well be written in a foreign language, the interpretations are so high flown and pragmatic. It belies the fact that all rock and its so-called Stars ever did was stand up and complain."

Van's bleary eyes swept the assembly, but his brain was sharpened by anger and bitterness.

"Chaps! Guys and gals! Pop-pickers! AOR! MOR! Punk Rock, Cock Rock, Heavy Metal, Black Brotherhoods, Disco Funk, my God it's even regarded as poetry. Compared to Eliot – Dylan Thomas; lines that have had every sense of English squeezed out of them.

"The Star appears and is recognized intuitively by all, like a messiah. He is spotted on a street corner and congratulated because he had the guts to say that the world isn't quite right. Hell's bells! When I say the world isn't quite right no one sends me a bloody fan letter. No blonde wunderfrau from Texas wobbles her tits at me. No one analyses my stance, testifies to my integrity. I AM THE TRUE MESSIAH! See? No one cares.

"And the poor Star who finds himself hounded from restaurant to doorstep, from telephone to mail box, from nightclub to dressing room, what of him? While I stand waiting for the blind to see, for the seekers of truth to scream for me, these dilettante pretenders are worshipped, an audience of millions hanging on their every word.

"And yet their words are ignored even while they are being cherished. The disciples expect their surrogate Napoleon to lead an army to make good their own dreams, reveries that are unique to each one because each one receives the communicated frustration and desperations of his leader with a different pair of interpretive ears, with a different heart.

"Stars are attributed with intelligence they don't have, beauty they haven't worked for, loyalty and love they are incapable of reciprocating, and strength they do not possess. Their lives are a short span within the lifetime of their admirers. They are treated like a beautiful vase of cut flowers. When wilted, simply replaced with new blooms. We never really try to get to know what it is that a Star is trying to say.

Why stand on a stage and sing and dance? Why proclaim such vainglorious notions as Peace on Earth, the Glory of Screwing on the Beach, and the Existence of God? Perhaps all they really want is attention and affection. All they can do is dance and make invitations to the Dance.

"What awaits the stelliform soul who, behind all this rabble-rousing, is a real being, with real talent? Some sycophant turns lunatic and blows his brains out! Spot the loony. He writes his letters in spidery handwriting, or types densely in capitals on both sides of A4 paper. He writes up the margins and adds five or six postscripts. He can't spell. He blames his school, his parents and a beautiful girl who once spurned him. God in heaven! Think of the misery created in a single street by a single beautiful girl who fails to notice the leering adoration of some pre-adolescent wanker passing her. Him and twenty others remembering her for the rest of their lives, recriminatory and bitter. Spot the loony! He says he has lived before – is living again once too often, I might add. Keep the sod away from me. I'll tell you what he looks like, he looks like a soul in torment, the type you might weep for. Quickly! Spot him! Before he blows your brains out!"

The anniversary dinner party was apparently over. Van got up and left without another word.

"As the wind builds up to a scream, the sound carrying across the valley and over the river, a fly brushes my cheek. I am lying in bed. The wind increases and turns on itself, crashing into the high embankment wall behind the house. My room shakes. The heat is full on but I still feel cold. In the middle of winter, flies seem to be revived by the greenhouse conditions I sleep in.

"Last night, half asleep, I awoke in a violent rage with buzzing in my ear. The *Daily Mirror* was all I had to hand. I got him in the end, swatting him against my pillow. I said a prayer for the little chap, moved by the sight of his innards.

"The wind is forcing its way between the tiny gaps around the windows to chill my face, yet I am still sweating. A body slips into bed beside me. It's my wife wearing her tight, black dress. She pushes her back up to my face and I gasp for breath. Starting out of a shallow sleep I realize she is just a spectre. I am not afraid."

On Tuesday morning an argument raged at the editor's desk.

". . . But this is for light-hearted, armchair reading. Why do you always have to commission lunatics? Celebrities are fine. But why the ghosts? What time does he get up in the morning? What pets does he have? What does he eat for breakfast? That's what our readers want."

The sub blanched, he had heard all this before. He nodded, turned, and went to phone his subject's publicist. He read the text at his own desk, drawing hard on a cigarette, feeling bored with the prospect of a rewrite.

"I believe our parents dictate our sleep patterns. The regime forced on my father by his work inverted night and day. As a musician, he was in bed early during the day, and up early in the evening. So it was with me. I wake up about four or five in the afternoon; at this time of the year I rise in darkness.

"I like to lie in bed in the morning. When my driver is held up on the motorway it gives me great pleasure. When I was drinking a lot I had brandy in my coffee to get me going. After a heavy binge I often took a large glassful straight. It made me feel normal. I often had massive breakfasts too. (When I have guests here I offer an impressive breakfast menu with kedgeree and kidneys and stuff. But they always opt for toast; there is no point pretending this is still old England.) Nowadays I simply suffer remembered hangovers, more painful than any I experienced in reality.

"I do my own tidying up afterwards, although I have a cleaner. I put last night's Horlicks cup in the machine. (Horlicks has replaced scotch as my bedtime ritual.) My driver will sip fresh coffee while I do this. He wonders why I can't live with a clockwork alarm like the rest of the world. The truth is, I need him there: if there is one time of the day I cannot abide to be alone, it's when I rise.

"At better times I might awake with a lover, hopefully the one I really care about. The trouble is that the good times are inextricably tangled with the bad. If I am on the wagon I become reclusive and antisocial. I tear out the phone or, if forced to answer, pretend that I'm too ill to move. So if there is a lover, they will have slept with a drunk.

"My days in London are not much use to anyone, but fun. I buy clothes, pop in to see friends and endure disturbing business appointments. Everyone is in the same boat: interest rates are running well over 22 per cent, I can't really catch up until they fall. In the evening I used to go and see a lot of bands, but at the moment I prefer a quiet dinner with a friend, and then a nightclub. People put up with me in these surroundings. In the public arena people are disturbed to see me consumed by nihilism, but among the truly futile I am invisible.

"I have an office which I rarely visit. My secretary is ready to quit. She's seen too much of my self-obliterative nature. I deal with personal mail at home. My wife, living separately (lucky thing), signs the bills. I have a studio, but most of the time other people use it. I suppose I get pleasure from that. Just now I can't work. Getting up so late, I have a short day. I live in a paradox: I feel comfortable with this unhappiness. I am content with misery.

"Living by the river, I can row and I do this frequently. I have a sun bed. I sit under it and listen to Radio 4. In the summer the garden is wonderful. I grow vegetables and prune fruit trees. I have an "estate manager" who rides around on a tractor and looks after things. I have a tennis court but no pool. I have a snooker table, but the lighting isn't right: you can only see two-thirds of the baize.

"I try to write every day. Solitude is vital. A week spent in town living at my club is totally lost. Once there I find it hard to leave. The room service, the friendly doormen and the brilliant barman who can make orange juice taste alcoholic conspire against me.

"I hate telephones unless it's me making the calls. Then I tend to go through my whole book, committing myself for months ahead. Living alone, what I find hardest to do is compose. To do this I need someone in the next room to disturb or stimulate.

"I don't do all my own shopping but I enjoy doing the big stuff: food for weekends and parties. I buy nearly all the good magazines and newspapers. Burning them at the end of the month is a long job. I have enjoyed this Christmas. I have pretended to have no money troubles and just lashed out for people. It's so much easier when you can first buy what you really want for yourself. Get that essential matter disposed of and then get down to trifles.

"I read about six books at once so I can adjust my reading to my mood. If I'm feeling delicate, I might read P. G. Wodehouse or H. E. Bates. If I feel strong, I'll tackle biographies. I have Robert Graves on at the moment. I read fairly heavy stuff. To mention all the authors might make me sound pretentious, so I won't, but I never read anything I don't enjoy. Every now and then, for a laugh, I listen to some music.

"In spurts I answer fan mail and business letters, play snooker, strum my guitar into a cassette machine, pray for forgiveness and think about what a total mess I've made of a life that had everything, and everyone, going for it."

The sub didn't bother to call the publicist. He made some cuts in the text, slashing out the maudlin bits, emphasizing the inconsequential details. This last page he screwed up and threw into the waste bin.

"And so, once more, to bed. The wind has stopped howling now. The bedroom is warm and inviting; the unread books piled high by the bedside like a promise. For a second I think about locking doors, but there is no point. I should feel insecure, but the truth is that if a burglar entered, I would probably sit him down, make him a drink and tell him to take what he wanted. But only after I'd bored him to death with my problems. There is only one thing here of value to take, and only I can take it.

"The cask of grief that cracks as I lie back always brings tears. Cool tears, spontaneous and free from self-pity, I think. I wonder about the kids of Toxteth and Brixton, and how hard are their lives. I thank God they don't know how absurdly I am wasting my own.

"Early in the morning? It's about three. I'm not tired. I'll read for two or three hours, then have a bath before I doze off properly. This ritual of lying down to sleep is just that, a ritual. Did I hear the buzz of a fly? Sometimes I imagine what it must be like to sleep where rats run, where insects crawl over you and into your coat, where the nightmarish visions are real and not delirium brought on by self-indulgence.

"What's the date? Does it matter? Nothing significant about today. What would I write if I were keeping a diary? *Didn't want to live any more*, or
I've always wanted to try it, just to see what it was like, or

This showed you, didn't it, you load of bastards? or
Please water the plants.

"I steel myself against approaching unpleasantness by thinking about eating slugs and enormous bluebottles; I imagine slashing my stomach and watching my guts emerge; I envisage a mirror image as I draw a rusty razor blade slowly across my throat from ear to ear. Then, simply swallowing a few tablets doesn't seem quite so bad. Please don't forget to water my plants."

The editor was at his desk, he took a slug of whisky as he read the edited transcript. He smiled grimly and sympathetically.

"This is better. Call his publicist once more and see if he can't get him to expand a little more on the gardening and rowing. With a few more cuts it will be okay. We don't know how much he sees of his family either. I like the insight into his relationship with his driver; that's very English, very Sunday. Yes, and the inherent theme of his will to overcome alcoholism. It's just what we want: a glimpse into the life of someone who, despite adversity, really enjoys living."

THE PLATE

September 3rd

I was a detective; brave and fearless. Like Sherlock I had my idiot partner. We called him Fan and he was black. I always listened carefully to whatever he said, then disregarded it. Why, at that point in my career, should I have even bothered with such buffoonery? I suppose I felt some pleasure in being snide. It all seems so long ago, like a previous life. I will explain everything soon, as best I can.

"Tell us again. Exactly what happened, for the Inspector." Fan talked to the girl indifferently as though he was dealing cards.

"Miss Lazenby," I said. She was a fairly plump girl of about twenty-three with blonde hair. Her face was weary, and small dark crescents capped her green eyes, which were hypnotizing and slightly reptilian. Her look was spell-binding and gave her heart away: she was sad, and she was sick. Behind those dilated pupils there was a mystery flashing that intrigued me. There was a call from her body that had me opening and closing my hands involuntarily. She did not appear beautiful at first – her chin was too petulant, her lips too thin and her hard eyes too widely spaced – but if you had a soul with a nose, you were sunk. I looked at my blotchy palm and the itching scar that ran from thumb to little finger. I turned the middle-aged hand over, and scratched instead the few hairs on the rivulet-veined skin.

"I'm sorry to have to take you through this again, but I assure you it will be helpful – most helpful. Of course we could continue without further questioning, but it's important that I, the senior detective here, should hear your story." Fan was smirking visibly as I spoke and I felt like hurling something at him.

"I told your friend here the poem." She started to talk suddenly and I leaned forward, obscenely obsequious. Already my mind was feeling the beginning of blood-lust.

"She didn't mention a poem, sir." Fan looked at the girl, poker-faced. She suddenly began to recite like an absent-minded schoolchild.

On a painted plate
My body lies, like an ornate pattern
On an ornate pattern;
A willow-story corpse in state.
My body lies on a painted plate.

The girl stopped, a fold of her blonde-streaked hair falling over one eye as she tried to light her cigarette. The noble Fan stretched over with a lighter. The flame was set so high she had to struggle to avoid being branded.

"Watch it!" I snapped.

He ignored me and stabbed another question at the girl: "What does this peculiar poem mean and where did you hear it?"

"He used to say it over and over."

"Who?"

"Robin, the boy who used to come to see me here, to bring my drugs. I'm not a heavy addict or anything, it was just the odd delivery of smoke or coke for parties. He was my boyfriend."

"Your pimp, you mean," Fan sneered.

God, I hated him. I couldn't bear to think that he might be right.

"I'm glad you're being so frank, miss," I said. "I'm sure it will help. Now, tell me again what you saw this morning."

The girl's mascara-smirched eyes cut into me and didn't soften for a second, but I could tell she was in bad shape. I was determined to help her get to the truth.

She began: "It was him. Robin. He was out there in the garden. He came back. I'd seen him in my imagination a thousand times. When the landlord came in and looked out he saw him too."

At this point she did crack and I had to rely on Fan to give me her complete story.

September 5th
Fan wanted me to forget the whole thing. Raston, the only other black detective in M Division, was brought in to interrogate the girl again. It was suggested I did nothing more. At first I capitulated, but listening to the girl's story again I only became more deeply convinced it was true.

Now I am here in the ceiling, locked deeply in love, holed up like a poisoned rat scuttering between floorboards as I die, shuffling the loose cork insulation chips lining the beams, whiskered nose covered in dust. I am steeped in fury, determined to make my mark, to win the day and the lady in distress. My back aches. My eye is glued to a hole in the ceiling of her room.

I still watch her. Two weeks ago I lost my job. I am no longer a commissioned detective. The landlord doesn't know this. I began my intimate surveillance soon after I was dismissed. I enter the building from the adjacent house, which her landlord also owns, into the roof via the attic door. Through a series of small holes I watch her. Now I am so desperately in love that I want to call out, or turn to snow and melt through the plaster into her hair.

Once, after watching her undress, pull aside her robe and ply the dusty hair between her legs with slow, pushing and pulsing finger-dances until she breathed and collapsed, I could restrain myself no longer. I wriggled from my secret place quite noisily, squeezed down through the attic door, down the staircase into the street, through the high-hedged garden full of weeds and flowers, and up to the adjacent house, knocking on the door, pushing the bell bearing her name.

She appeared on the balcony above me. "What the hell do you want?" she shouted.

"I need to talk to you." I lied. "I have learned something."

I scratched my palm and looked at my scuffed shoes and chalky clothing. The landlord had come to the door, and stood looking at me as I looked up at the balcony where she had been. I studied it as a sacred spot, appreciating the cracked and eroded stone, crumbling and green in places. (It was Raston who got me dismissed. He and Fan had done some very cursory investigation, but they never really believed the girl's story. I did. I believed it as though I had lived it, and neglected every other case I was ordered to follow up, until it all got out of hand. The only consolation was that Raston himself quit when a full investigation was threatened. I wanted the truth, for me – and the girl.)

She arrived downstairs, her robe drawn around her. Her face glowed and she seemed more beautiful than I had ever seen her. I thought I smelt a fleeting scent of female sex. Perhaps it was my imagination, but it sent me into a dizzy, spiralling sparrow-hawk glide from which I thought I couldn't recover.

She immediately tore into me: "What the bloody hell do you want? Why don't you bastards ever leave me alone? I'm sorry I even told you about all this."

Her eyes were crisp slits, and her hands were shaking. With a boyish memory I climbed the boughs of a wind-blown tree far too high; exhilarating, dangerous, no way up or down. She had to let me in. I think tears may have filled my eyes, or the earnestness I tried to communicate may have penetrated – I'm not sure. We went to her room. I knew it so well. I knew exactly where to sit.

October 2nd

Lying here now, in the roof, looking through the little hole next to the place where the rose of the lamp hangs through the ceiling, I can see where I sat. I don't know why I am even thinking of telling this story. I can't tell now whether the things I said to her were lies or truth, whether what I write here is what I remember of what happened, or pieces of fact and fiction.

Why have I humiliated myself? Why have I degraded the love I feel for her?

After the first interrogation I had grabbed Fan and walked into the street full of flying paper and filthy children. I had felt confused but resolved never to go home again. After a few hours' work at the station I went to the Common and smelt the trees and listened to the rush-hour traffic in the middle distance. I kissed every living thing. From afar I watched faces; each one seemed attractive and belonging in some way, old and young.

All I saw in my mind was that fold of hair, that shaking hand, her eyes as cold as a snake's, and from each a strange tear frozen against her smudged mask of make-up. Probably a dozen times I have watched her wake up in shafts of sunlight, sheet to one side, her breasts floating with the tiniest movement of breath, her hand always touching her sex in sleep. How I cursed the winter when the morning light came too late, when I strained to see her in the darkness. I hardly ate or slept, I didn't dare, I might have missed a second of some new movement, some special action from my precious tragedienne.

Once I saw a man in her room. I had become so excited I didn't know whether to die there and then. I hated him so desperately. He had been black. (No, it wasn't Fan or Raston.) She was a diffident lover. She'd lain on the sofa, legs spread, awaiting him and he'd thrust into her with little real attention to himself or her. He took at least an hour and a half to come. My own centre, veined and blood-flooded, felt the length of two palms. In their dismal hour and a half I came three times. The black man had thrown money to her before he left.

I sat down on the same sofa.

"Well?" she demanded. "What have you found out?"

So close to her, filled with the smell of her in the room she had lived in for months, I wanted to be sucked into her womb then and there. Her legs were tightly crossed, her robe pulled over her like steely armour. She seemed to be ready to resist anything I told her.

"Please listen to what I have to say. I'm sorry to bother you with this, it might not mean a thing, but I need to know." My slashed palm and once broken fingers itched and ached.

"I was following up a very tenuous lead – one of the names of Robin's friends you mentioned – I was watching a club in the factory area behind the railway, Yard Street. It's well known as an area where pushers operate. On several nights the same thing happened. A large old car would pull up in the street, and the driver would get out, without being furtive, and go into the club. He was about five-eight, with bleached hair, but normally dressed. About ten minutes later the boot of the car would open, and out would struggle about three or four kids – not always the same kids as far as I could see – they were differently dressed each time. They were always brightly turned out, with extreme make-up. On one occasion they looked like punks of the old order, belts and chains, their faces pale, but very carefully painted . . ."

The girl was getting interested. She shifted, leaned forward.

"On another occasion people emerged from the boot of the car dressed in rags like tramps, but again their faces were made up so delicately that each one was beautiful, and hard to identify. Once they were wearing flowing gowns and suits, then military coats, sashed and emblazoned, but worn with shoes like children's woollen slippers. Then the hair would be long and flowing on the males, shaved to the scalp on the girls. Then the girls might have hair like wire attached to their scalps, their men Aryan or like ancient Yehudis, with earlocks and scruffy gaberdine suits . . ."

Was I lying? I was at least keeping her attention.

". . . but always this incredible make-up, so carefully applied, as though by some fantastic theatrical expert. The whole affair is totally confusing."

The girl was up and pacing. Her hips swung beneath the robe, her hair, pulled into a rough pony-tail behind her head, tossed as she pulled on her cigarette.

I broke the short silence: "Did you know my friend Raston quit the force over this case?"

The girl whirled on me, almost sneering. "Why should I know? Why should I care?"

"No, no – I didn't mean because of you or anything. He quit because he felt I was going too far, he was worried by my actions, he said I was becoming obsessed. I wouldn't let him work on anything else. He put in a protest and I threatened to have him sacked for indiscipline. He quit."

"Am I beholden to you then? Jesus Christ! Someone once lectured me about the danger of nuclear war. She spouted on about how little warning we will get. What I need is a bloody two-minute warning from the likes of her, and you, and the rest – bloody hell, here I am with an aching habit, no one will deal with me any more, you had the bloody house under observation for so long. All my friends think I'm barmy . . ."

"I believe you." I was playing my only real card.

She stopped walking, her arms dropped to her sides. She fell into the sofa like a discarded child-doll. Tears flooded over her face even though her expression remained that of a cynical, frozen mannequin.

I went on: "I want to protect you – I'm worried about these people. I'm sure they park their car just over the road. It's there for an hour or more sometimes – yet I know there are probably at least three, sometimes four, people dressed like tops squashed into the boot! There must be some connection!"

She stared at me blankly.

I hurried on: "I want you to let me watch from this room for a few nights. You can sleep in the back room. I will keep out of your way."

"No!" She put her hand under her robe and scratched her breast. "Yes – yes, all right."

The girl had told Fan that she had seen her boyfriend, Robin, murdered in the garden outside her home in a strange and ritual killing. She had said that three men had dragged this man Robin into the garden where she had heard his cries. The men were dressed at the very height of the latest fashion of the time, a romantic look, long gowns over flowing trousers, almost like Arabs, hair Hitler-youth, faces made up white with a single line from ear to nose on the left side of the face. They had stabbed him repeatedly, then left. The part of her story that made Fan question her sanity was her claim that the attackers had then squeezed into the boot of a car and were driven away. They took the man's body with them.

She had said nothing to anyone until early morning. On the day we met, she had looked from her balcony and seen Robin's pale, decaying body laid out on an absurdly large china plate in the middle of the garden. By the time she had found her sense of balance, bringing the landlord up with her screams, the vision – or reality – had vanished. The poem Robin had often repeated to her had suddenly manifested itself. At first the landlord corroborated this second part of her story. I think he changed his mind when he realized how absurd it sounded.

October 9th

Of course, everything I've written is in fact true. I was a detective and I have now lost my job. All that has happened since is that I am convinced that I am losing my mind over this, my infatuation with the Lazenby girl, but there is nothing I can do. She depends on me a little now. That is precious to me. At least I no longer sleep in the garret.

October 13th

She hates me. I love her. I am back in the roof again. I annoyed her. The landlord let me have the room below the attic area I use to observe her and I can now see the street. I'm still very confused about the young people getting out of the car boot in Yard Street. I can see it so clearly I feel sure it must have happened. Yes, of course it happened; it just seems too incredible to be true. But it does add substance to her story. My relating that single event to her was what persuaded her to allow me into her flat for those few weeks. To confront her on the stairs was all I dreamed of. To say hello. The sun is shining.

In my new room in the house next door I made some coffee.
As I poured the water over the grounds in the filter it all
overflowed, black and gritty. I took a cloth and started to
wipe it away. The coffee clung to the rag, and on each
successive sweep dry grounds fell over the area I had wiped.
I became infuriated and hurled the rag and the muck to one
side. As I gazed at the mess on the scratched wooden table,
inspiration hit me.

I rang some agencies and told them I was planning to make
a short surrealist film. Once I had sketched out my idea they
rang off, promising to call back. They never did. I tried some
villains, contacts from the past. Again, once I had told them
my plan they slunk away across the billiard halls laughing
behind their hands. Nothing gives a villain as much pleasure
as a fallen copper. They all thought I was doing drugs or
something, but I had simply been inspired. I just needed a
few people to help.

For a few evenings I visited Yard Street again. I was doing
a recce. I stood in the shadows and watched the kids arriving.
I hoped to see the car-boot crew. The whole idea was, of
course, peculiar but still I waited. It didn't occur to me that
the girl's story might have changed as a result of what I had
said I'd seen. She was an addict on the slope, after all. I
remember a friend of mine on the Force telling me that when
an addict, of their own volition, elected to go to a clinic for a
cure their friends called the act "going to the police". The
apophthegm made me feel warm inside when I repeated it to
myself.

People arrived and left. The clothes some of them had the
courage to wear at night were astounding. Sometimes, amid
the young and vital explosion of colourful dress, there might
loiter an older man in dress clothes or a woman in an evening
gown. Somehow they would be absorbed without looking
out of place. That was something notable about these kids –
their outfits were so various that they absorbed anyone and
everything. After a couple of nights I gave up.

October 30th

I am back in the attic. She never goes out. Sometimes she watches the television late at night with the sound turned off. The sofa is ragged, one arm falling away, the stuffing pulled out in a heap on the floor. A tribal rug, appearing to be moth-eaten and burned with cigarette holes, hangs on one wall. Her robe is perpetually hanging open, her naked body so familiar to me now that I can open and shut my eyes and see, and feel, every inch of her. I've watched her pick at her nails and her nose for hours on end, so insistently that a sudden flood of blood has rushed over her hand and she has leapt up in horror, thrusting a tissue to her nostrils. I've watched her pull up her leg at an angle and rub her toes, squeeze them together, the toenails uneven, or too wide. She has then cut delicately at them with tiny scissors. With her legs spread widely apart I have seen her clitoris, the lips of her vulva.

I fall asleep watching her. I dream of strolling by the side of a dark canal and meeting a man walking a dog. As they pass, I turn and look after them, the dog's behind is her exquisite cunt, moist and rouged. In sleep the sudden scent of lavender, invaded by a pervasion of sex, floods through my sleep-starved brain. Starting awake I hear a car horn in the street. I go down and look out of the window. There is a car outside and the horn sounds again. Looking through one of the peepholes back in the attic, I see she has heard. Still awake she is sitting cross-legged on the craggy sofa, gazing at the silent TV screen, but she doesn't move.

Now when I watch her she seems to have a golden aura. Perhaps it's because I'm letting myself get so deeply tired. Or maybe it's just the phenomenon that occurs whenever you stare too long at something. I remember as a child that I loved to scare myself after the vibrancy of a hot bath by gazing into my own eyes, my hair swept back, my face reflected in the mirror. I would stare and stare until my face started to become recognizable as the face of an animal. I remember the distortions vividly: my nose bent and blotchy; my eyes like bloody gashes; the eyeballs, never still, like oscillating slugs caught in an oily bath, the tiny hairs and blemishes on my face enlarged and mobile; my hands ugly when held up beside my face.

It would feel unendurable, but for some masochistic reason I endured it, almost recoiling in revulsion at the unfamiliar vision that I knew was my own face. Then, after about ten minutes, everything would clear and become peaceful. I would end my mirror-gazing, a ten-year-old boy looking at the face of his own father. One quick blink and everything returned to normal. It had just been an illusion.

It felt like a unique power. I could carry myself safely through an appalling hallucination and then pull myself rapidly and confidently back to secure reality. My whole life had become such a dangerous game.

The furtiveness of my position is a peculiar delight to me. I like the deceit, and the feeling of true subterfuge. I never feel claustrophobic as long as she is in the room below, as long as my eyes are on her. The peephole I have arranged over her bed is in a far corner of the attic, well under the eaves. When looking there I can sometimes hardly breathe, but as long as I can see her in the dim yellow light from the street lamps, I feel as though I'm on an ocean. There is nothing she can do that makes her look unpleasant to me. When I gaze at her at length, keeping my eyes open without blinking, just as I did as a boy gazing at my reflection, she seems to become ever more pure and transparent. Her skin glows and her eyes wish through their half-closed lids, perhaps recalling memories of wafting trees. Her hair, always falling and moving, seems to become liquid.

The pain of my love for her is beyond all words. It is the most unbearably delicious sensation, but agonizing and despicable. My chest feels pitted as though by the boot heel of a Cossack, my face burn-scarred by the iron of an inquisitor. There is no torture I have not endured, none I would refuse to undergo, in order to remain close to her. If a miraculous potion was forced to my lips that made me forget her forever, that flooded me instead with a conventional ecstasy, that made me feel as though I sat at the feet of God Himself, surrounded by hosts of angels, bathed in celestial music, if I was released from pain, then ironically I would scream for ever. I would know intuitively that I had lost something more precious than an eternity of bliss: the exquisite pain of separation from some unknown object of my desire, more attractive than the gravity of the centre of the universe itself.

I stood outside the door of her house for the first time in over a week. I rang her bell just as the landlord came up the path behind me carrying a bag of groceries.

"If you're calling for the Lazenby girl, you can give her these."

He didn't even pass them to me. He placed them beside me and walked in, leaving the door open for me. She had, as usual, not responded to the bell. I craned up at her balcony. She didn't appear. I rang once more and waited. The balcony doors were open and the tatty lace curtains blew slowly back and forth. I picked up the bag and went up the stairs. Outside her door I waited and listened. I could hear nothing. From under it, daylight from the open window shone over my feet. I felt I wanted to bend down and bathe my hands in the sacred light, gather it up and fill my pockets with it, drench myself in it. Finally I knocked. She opened the door. I spoke: "I've lost my job, you know." I don't know why I said this: I couldn't even remember whether I had already told her.

"Come in," she said, taking the groceries from my arms. As she turned and walked to the little kitchen in the back of the room, I realized this was the first time I had seen her wearing anything other than the robe. She was in a blue dress. I have never seen a blue like it: it glowed, carrying an energy like the blue of the summer sky.

"Thank you for bringing up the groceries. Did he leave them downstairs?" She turned to face me as she took things out of the bag. Her eyes were carefully made up. She was wearing make-up on her skin too; deep, slightly sparkling blusher accentuated her cheekbones and temples. Her lips shone and glittered, her teeth sparkled moistly.

"Yes. Does he help you?" I gestured at the groceries. I sat on the sofa and put both hands on it, sensuously feeling the surface of the cushions.

"I never go out. He gets them for me. Always. I can't go out. Why did you lose your job?"

She knew why. I felt so close to her, so familiar to her, that I almost exploded at her with the licence of a familiar lover. I wanted to enjoy a tiff, to explore dangerous territory, then collapse into forgiving embraces. I caught her dispassionate, enquiring look and came to.

"I lost it because of you. Because of the case, I mean."

The stiffening I had expected from her never came. She calmly carried on putting tins into a high cupboard, and I looked at her back. Her shoulders. Her spine. The soft material of the blue dress was simply there. I was feeling ever more daring, I mouthed her name: "Rhea."

As I spoke, the sudden rush of impatience and irritation I had anticipated arrived in her. She laid down a food packet on the ledge below the shelves and looked at her hands. She leaned forward on both arms, her shoulders hunched up slightly. When she finally spoke I could hear that she was crying. Her question began low, rising in pitch and intensity almost to a doodlebug scream. "Why, why – please tell me why you won't leave me alone?"

At the end of the question she slammed the doors of the cupboard, but they flew open again and one of them hit her on the face. When she turned to me, black streaks of mascara ran down her rouged face, blood trickled from her left cheekbone, a gash about half an inch long gaped below her eye.

"Fuck it. Why do you keep coming here? What the fuck do you want?" She took a step towards me and I was scared. I had never been as scared of a woman before.

"It's your story, I just can't get it out of my mind. You know I believe it, just as you told it." I was blathering.

Wiping at one side of my neck I felt an icy warmth. It felt like blood. I surreptitiously looked at my hand to check. It was sweat. She was the bloodied one. "Your face," I said, "it's cut quite badly, you know."

She slumped into a chair by the sink and grabbed a small, dirty mirror that sat behind the water taps.

"Oh, screw it!" She dabbed at her face with the cuff of the blue dress. It seemed sacrilegious to me.

"Here – use my hanky." I pulled it out but it was filthy.

She didn't even look up from the mirror. "Listen, just piss off, will you? Go. I've got a visitor coming. Thanks for bringing up the groceries."

She glanced up for a second. I hesitated, then moved to the door. She spoke when I was halfway out. "Why did you move in next door? Are you spying on me?"

She looked up and I faced her. My arms, already by my sides, slumped as I answered, "Yes."

November 3rd

I've become a worm. Not a beetle, but a worm. Little point in spying any more: the girl is in a mental hospital somewhere. Landlord told me, loving every minute of it.

November 17th

Today I saw her come home. She was with her mother. I don't think she saw me. I feel elated. The landlord sneers as he sees me scurrying back into my flat. Maybe he knows. I must be careful. Now she knows I spy on her. I admitted it. What a bloody fool.

Her mother put her into bed this morning, left for the day, and is back now. I want her to go away.

November 24th

For weeks now I have waited. The girl does not seem to be getting any better.

I couldn't wait any longer to find out how she was and stopped her mother in the street.

"How is Rhea? I'm a friend."

"She is very confused. She thinks she is crazy." Her mother stopped before walking down the path to the house. She looked at me carefully. "How do you know her?"

"I was a police officer assigned to her case." I tried to seem natural and assured.

"It is you people who are to blame."

"Why is that?" I asked defensively.

"Because you believed her absurd story at first, then didn't follow it up. You have made her believe she is crazy. What about the landlord? Didn't he corroborate her story?"

"At first – yes," I agreed, "but there was a lot of confusion. I left the Force. Then the case was taken over by another man who also left the Force. Finally it was dropped. In the end your daughter changed her story. We think she did it so it would fit a poem of her boyfriend's. I was trying to help her when she cracked up."

Her mother responded immediately. "It was you who was spying on her?"

"Of course I wasn't spying on her. She was delirious, upset." I wondered if I looked as red as I felt.

The woman seemed impatient with me then, and went inside.

November 26th

I have decided that I will help the girl. I will definitely carry out my inspired plan to re-enact the story as she first told it to Fan six weeks ago. I have managed to get some out-of-work actors together. I have cut the back seat out of an old car and tomorrow I am going to shock her out of her depression. I want her, but I am still so much a copper I also want the truth. I feel sure she told me what she thought was the truth, or what was close to the truth. When she sees again what she thinks she imagined, she will remember everything, she will tell me all. Then I can help her.

That night I couldn't help but spy on her again. She lay sweating and naked on her bed, her breasts rolled, and her belly, a little heavier since her mother had been feeding her every day, lolled from side to side as she tossed and turned. Asleep she was more beautiful, I think, than any woman I have ever seen, and her skin became transparent and luminous. Her hair fell into strands over her face. She nearly always slept with her legs wide apart, her cunt covered in hair that spread a little way inside her thighs and generously over her lower belly. Whenever I watched her for very long, tears would fill my eyes. I had stopped masturbating while looking at her; it seemed wrong. She was too much a beloved ikon to me, even when naked like this. When morning came I went to bed for a few hours' sleep. The actors would be around at midday.

Everything had been rehearsed. It was simple: they were to put on the various costumes I had provided. One of them, a younger man, was to do the make-up for the four others. The actor who was to play the corpse tried on his trick death-knife and monkeyed around on the floor pretending to die. The plate, which was to be fashioned from an old circular table top I had picked up at a junk shop, was to be delivered to the garden at four that afternoon. At 4.30 I knocked at her door.

"Who is it?" Her mother's voice.

"It's me."

She opened the door and let me in. The girl was in bed, looking radiant. I bowed and scraped. "I hope you are feeling better, Miss Lazenby."

"What the fuck do you want?" she sneered.

"Rhea!" rebuked her mother. "How dare you? This young man is concerned about you. At least you can be polite." She turned to me. "I'm sorry. I know you are a friend and you understand what she's been through. Talk to her quietly for a minute. It will help her. I'll go and make some tea."

I went over to the bed and sat on the chair beside it. The girl looked at me sideways and started to laugh.

I was starting to feel worse. "Please don't laugh at me. I really want to know how you are," I stuttered.

She seemed hurt by this request. The smile turned to tears; suddenly she put her face into my lap and lay across my body shuddering with sobs. I held her beautiful head in my hands and thanked God for the moment. Then she said something I hardly heard or understood:

"Apart from losing the baby and finding out I had cancer, everything has fallen into place beautifully."

It was so pathetic, so moving, that I had to fight off my tears. She became silent, her face still in my lap. Her sighs were deep and distant. I didn't dare to ask what baby or what cancer she was talking about. I turned her face up to mine and touched the spot below her eye where she had bled.

"It's healed okay," she said. She looked straight at me. I leaned down and raised her face towards mine. Just as my lips touched hers the pre-arranged car horn sounded from the street outside. She ignored it and pulled my hesitant mouth back on to hers and kissed me deeply.

"I'm happy now, with you I'm happy — I know you love me. The doctors told me that it was having too many sexual partners that brought on the cancer. It was down there," she pushed at her belly, "and it was the junk that made me lose Robin's baby. I just went crazy, totally crazy, but I'm happy now."

The car horn sounded again, this time for a full ten seconds. My actors were ready to play. The plate was in the garden. Robin's "body" was spread out on it, a knife in the chest. As soon as she appeared at the window my troupe would drag the body away and all climb into the car through the boot. They would then drive away. The horn sounded again and Rhea got up to cross to the window. Just then her mother walked back into the room, cooing, "Everything's fine now. Tea for you two and everything's fine."

I am a child. Yesterday my mother was distracted and wanted to make a pact. She wants to divulge to me the name of her secret love: the true object of her highest devotion and desire. In return she wants to teach me to ride.

I tried to tell mother about my dream. She stopped me. She said I could tell her everything and anything I wished, I could even bore her, but she didn't want to be patronized. All of a sudden I was feeling sick. Then she said that there was one thing I could tell her nothing about that she didn't already know. It was horses. She said I wasn't to try to tell her anything new about horses.

Our telephone keeps getting crossed lines. Today I overheard two women. I wonder if they knew I was listening. I still don't quite understand what they were talking about, but I don't think I dare ask my mother. I would go red because while I was listening I was aroused; my mother is very intuitive about things like that. I'll just keep it to myself. I'll forget all about it. I'll tell the only boy in our class who is really in the know about girls.

They were leaving long pauses in their conversation. One woman would let out a great sigh, and the other would say something intimately, as though she was trying to titillate her friend. She kept on saying the same sentence: "I rode him – just like a horse."

I'll tell my friend about it. He'll explain. Then I'll forget all about it. I wish I could ask my mother about it now. Perhaps I could just tell the truth: say I got a crossed line and heard what the woman said. But it's something secret and rude. I know it is. My mother would wonder why I carried on listening. I'd be embarrassed. I'll just have to wait to tell my friend.

Perhaps I can learn to overcome my fear of riding by studying in secret? I will build a hobby horse. Then I can sit astride it, mount it, tumble from it and learn all the tricks without embarrassment. One day I will emerge from my hide-out and shock everyone with my fantastic ability. Then perhaps people who think little of me will stop and stare in amazement.

I'll get extra respect and attention from my parents too, because in their eyes I will appear more beautiful when I am astride a great horse.

Why am I ashamed to let anyone know I am afraid? What's wrong with fear?

My mother used to come to see me when I was at school by the seaside. Her leaving always hurt terribly. I could never talk about it. In later years, during holidays and weekends, we had a little mare in the paddock. Just having it there was utter bliss for me. I was surrounded then by all the females I loved the most. But as the years passed I realized it was the little foal I loved best. It was a forbidden love. Once, in desperation, I tried to ride the animal, but I felt like a wretch; I simply couldn't do it.

Now the foal is rarely here. But when she does appear she comes like the sun, a prodigal from a distant colony. Her beauty always strikes me, but there's more – it's a familiarity I feel. Sometimes I sense that the foal has always belonged to me. I've never been jealous of her other riders. I've known that it's really only my love that will satisfy her.

I miss her so terribly. I admit I don't always dream of her, but that's agonizing because it feels like treachery. I can never have her, never ride her or break her. This obsession of mine is unfair to everyone, but mostly to her. For she has everything to gain: no one on earth who has ever lived, lives now or shall live can love her or adore her as I do.

So you see, my story is much like yours. I have a mother whom I loved more than I ever knew; sometimes I thought that love had turned to hate, but it hadn't. I have a father whom I respected and idealized above all others; now I see he is just a man, I respect him among others. I have had friends whom I abused and who abused me; all that has become neutralized. I now have a wife and I have children; I hope that saying they are part of my life doesn't deny them freedom.

I am very ordinary. I have made mistakes and found it hard to forgive myself, just like you.

What value can there be in the handshake of a man who has coldly broken the most important contract he is ever likely to make in his life?

I still believe in God. I've pushed all thoughts of him aside, but he is still on my case. I sound conceited but I think I'm special. Why should I pretend otherwise? If I'm not special, then I must be unusually lucky, and if I'm that lucky with no talent and no guardian angel, then that makes me special. I'm being careless, but I must take this route. I know in my bones I'm right.

Shivering slightly, and feeling feverish, I pushed the paddock gate open. I knew I was not going to hesitate. I walked deliberately forward and the foal stirred from her standing sleep. Before she was completely awake I threw myself on to her back and hung on to her neck. I suddenly felt I should have first taken off my clothes, but I just sat there. The little horse didn't move. I was afraid I had frightened her and tried to soothe her. I stroked her, cooing: "Don't worry, don't worry."

After a few minutes I felt too warm, and dismounted. I slipped off my trousers and shirt. It felt delicious to be naked in the early morning air and the sensation was cutting through my hangover. I stood up against the little mare's body and stroked her mane. Suddenly, I heard someone walking in the lane nearby and picked up my clothes and ran back to the house.

For a while I was convinced that the horse in my dreams and memories was in some way a symbol connected with an opium-drenched past life. I was wrong. The horse I feared to ride was a real giant, not a circus clown's prop.

But I have to be careful. I must not end up like a detective who tries to make the facts fit his own idea of who is guilty. I've been concocting fabulous, imaginative fairy tales, hoping that they might lead me to what really happened.

Given the truth just once, I would hardly know what to do with it.

Out in the street a little seven-year-old boy is wandering in the afternoon sunlight. There is no one else in sight. He kicks stones into the river, his hands are in his pockets. He has blonde hair; a very pretty child.

Suddenly, I feel afraid for him: if he were a little girl of the same age, he wouldn't be allowed to roam free by the riverside. How things have changed since I was like him. I've never been afraid to walk in the street.

What a terrible fate it is to be young. To be faced with life's razor-edged pathway, a withheld freedom in any case, only safe for the strong or ugly.

So beauty is rarely seen; youth is rarely at liberty; fear becomes a discipline, once again, for the frail and the beautiful.

And what of the misfits? We are able to roam free. We observe and become commentators and artists. Our freedom is absolute.

It's a bitter irony, then, that the beautiful have come to be envious of the ugly just as the frail covet the freedom of the strong.

LAGUNA. VALENTINE'S DAY, 1982

A white wall curves into the distance. It disappears before the brittle, unrefracted light can absorb it. There is no sun; this brilliance shines from the whole sky and I make no shadow. About every half-mile there is an open archway in the wall. I sit in a small armchair upholstered in an understated flower pattern and contemplate the view. Before me stretches a vast, shining beach covered with dry sand. There is no wind. In the distance I can see the edge of an ocean that stretches away to a horizon that seems unusually high and straight. I am on a big planet.

There is silence. I don't hear the tinkling celestial sounds I used to hear in the gardens through the door behind me. This is not what I thought Paradise would look like. No one emerges through the other, distant doorways I can see. Strange. All of us believed we were trapped inside that tormenting place of change and strain. Yet the doors are open. I didn't need a key. I just walked through.

What now? In the distance I can see two tiny figures on horses by the water's edge. They are throwing up spray as they ride towards me. I will go and meet them. I get up from the comfortable armchair I have been sitting in and walk forward, and as I do so the wall behind me recedes rapidly. From a distance I can now hear the noises of music, dancing, fighting, bombs, laughing, screaming and copulation. I am walking away.

The flat, hard sand beneath my feet feels like glass, and though I have walked quite a long time I don't seem to be any nearer the water's edge. The riders in the distance are much closer now, and I can see that they have a mount for me on a rein. It is a white horse. As the riders get nearer I realize, without any shame, that I am naked and my phallus is erect and enormous, like Dionysus.

The riders have pulled up a good hundred yards off. They wave, but I can't see who they are. A young couple, wearing check shirts and riding boots. They look like a handsome pair. The man releases the white horse and slaps it and it starts to walk towards me. Then the couple turn their steeds and ride back to the surf; they appear to ride straight into the sea, churning up the water. Eventually they are submerged and, as the white horse reaches me, the last widening ripple they have created shimmers to a stop.

The horse is beautiful. Its mane is flowing and clean, its coat brushed and smooth. Its eyelashes are long and curved. The horse is now before me, it bares its teeth and its tongue flicks out. I hold the great, gorgeous head in my hands. Then I walk behind the beautiful creature and, brushing aside the tail, slide deeply into it.

When my orgasm comes it is without sensation. I am no longer an animal. My phallus diminishes and my horse flicks its tail and stands on its back legs, magnificent. When it crashes down on the sand it bares its teeth once again and then licks my cheek. I grab its mane and pull myself up. We are suddenly and rapidly off at a canter. At last I can ride. I am in perfect control. I urge the horse into a gallop and the wind cools my face. I am riding towards the water's edge.